Dr Tim Benson is Britain's leading authority on political cartoons. He runs the world's largest gallery for original pen-and-ink political and satirical cartoons. He has produced numerous books on the history of cartoons, including *David Low Censored*, *Suezcide: A Cartoon History of the Suez Crisis*, *Giles's War*, *Churchill in Caricature*, *Low and the Dictators*, *The Cartoon Century: Modern Britain through the Eyes of its Cartoonists*, *Drawing the Curtain: The Cold War in Cartoons*, *Over the Top: A Cartoon History of Australia at War*, *How to be British: A Cartoon Celebration*, *Churchill: A life in Cartoons* and over ten volumes of *Britain's Best Political Cartoons.*

This book is dedicated to my great-great-grandfather Peysach Czyzyk who was orphaned at the age of three as a result of a Russian Pogrom.

DRAWN TO THE PROMISED LAND

A CARTOON HISTORY OF BRITAIN, PALESTINE AND THE JEWS: 1917–1949

TIM BENSON

HALBAN
LONDON

First published in Great Britain by
Halban Publishers Ltd.
2024

www.halbanpublishers.com

A CIP catalogue record for this book is available from the British Library.

ISBN 978 1 912600 15 1

The author wishes to thank Warren Bernard and Dr Ulrich Schnakenberg for their help in researching images for this anthology. The author would also like to thank Steve Bright for colourising the cartoon on the front cover and restoring two of the cartoons.

Book design by Dan Yates

Printed in Great Britain by
CPI Group (UK) Ltd, Croydon CR0 4YY

INTRODUCTION

From the end of the eighteenth century, the vast majority of European Jews were restricted to living in what was known as the 'Pale of Settlement' under Russian rule. This was a stretch of land, mainly in western Russia, central and eastern Poland, the Baltic States and Ukraine, which spread from the Baltic Sea down to the Black Sea. Although Jews were allowed to live and trade in the 'Pale', they were still subject to severe restrictions and suffered under antisemitic policies. Tensions escalated with the assassination of Tsar Alexander II in 1881, for which many falsely blamed the Jews. Three years of violent pogroms ensued. Thousands of Jews were killed and their homes destroyed. In response, thousands more Jews left for Western Europe, South Africa and the United States, and some to Palestine. The Austrian journalist Theodor Herzl believed only a Jewish national state would allow Jews to live in peace and security. In 1897 he assembled the first Zionist Congress in Basel, which agreed that Zionism would create 'for the Jewish people a home in Palestine secured by public law'. As a consequence, greater numbers of ideologically driven younger Jews emigrated to Palestine, spurred on by the dream of establishing a Jewish state in their ancestral homeland.

Until its capture by the British during the latter stages of the First World War, Palestine had proved itself of little interest to political cartoonists. The obvious deduction is that they believed the Ottoman's four-century rule was unimportant to their readers either within the British Empire or in the United States. This is surprising, considering Britain was then very much a practising Christian country and Palestine had always been of great religious significance not only to Muslims and Jews, but also to Christians. Consequently, I struggled to source cartoons on the subject of Palestine prior to November 1917 – that also

Stop Your Cruel Oppression of the Jews

President Theodore Roosevelt reprimands Tsar Nicholas II:
'Now that you have peace without, why not remove his burden and have peace within your borders?'

Repeated murderous pogroms by Tsar Nicholas II increasingly angered American opinion. President Roosevelt forwarded a petition to the Tsar calling on him to stop the persecution of Jews. The Tsar rejected it and the pogroms continued. Consequently, hundreds of thousands of Jews continued to flee Russia.

Emil Flohri, *Judge* (United States)
September 1904

being the month when the British government announced the Balfour Declaration. On 2 November 1917, in a letter to Lord Rothschild, British Foreign Secretary Arthur Balfour pledged to help establish a national home for the Jewish people in Palestine. This momentous statement of intent would soon have wide-ranging repercussions for Britain and the Middle East. However, like Palestine, the 'Declaration' was also considered at the time un-newsworthy by most cartoonists, who simply ignored it. This was understandable as the British public was preoccupied by what was happening on the Western Front, the war now being in its fourth earth-shattering year. Ever-increasing casualty lists and little to no sign of a significant breakthrough meant that the priority for cartoonists was to give the 'Hun' and the 'Turk' a good daily bashing in order to raise their readers' morale. Not one cartoon on the Balfour Declaration appeared in any of the main national dailies. The only two references I found were after Jerusalem had been captured by the British in December 1917. One appeared in the *Western Mail*, published in Cardiff (p.7), and the other in the *British Sentinel*, a minor publication (*right*). The press in the United States were even less interested, with none of the national or state newspapers commenting either. However, I did miraculously find two cartoons on the subject from the New York Jewish press, which at the time was published in Yiddish. Interestingly, the cartoons were both suspicious of British intentions rather than celebratory.

In mitigation, and in contrast to North America, very few British newspapers of 1917 carried daily political cartoons. The broadsheets such as *The Times*, the *Manchester Guardian* and the *Daily Telegraph*

The War, 'A Door of Hope' to the Wandering Jew
Cartoonist Unknown, *British Sentinel*
December 1917

did not have cartoons because they considered them too frivolous an item for a serious newspaper. It was not until the 1960s that the broadsheets began to employ political cartoonists. By contrast, the national tabloids, such as the *Daily Mail, Daily Dispatch, Daily Graphic, Western Mail, News of the World* and the *Daily Express*, did employ full-time cartoonists, as did a number of the London evening papers. However, by 1917, three national tabloids had stopped carrying cartoons because their staff cartoonists had enlisted in the army. Strube at the *Daily Express* and Wyndham Robinson at the *Morning Post* had both joined the Artists Rifles in 1915, and by 1917 were serving on the Western Front. In May 1917, the *Daily Herald*'s Will Dyson was commissioned and became Australia's first official war artist attached to the Australian Imperial Force in France. Political cartoons could also be found at the time in satirical magazines such as *Punch, The Bystander, John Bull, London Opinion* and *Passing Show*, to name but a few. They all had regular contributions by established artists. Like their counterparts on the newspapers, *Punch* cartoonists Ernest Shepard, Burt Thomas, Kenneth Bird ('Fougasse') and Bruce Bairnsfather, who drew for *The Bystander*, had also enlisted in the British Army and were fighting in France.

In comparison to the lack of coverage given to the Balfour Declaration, the British Army's exploits in kicking the Turks out of Palestine and the capture of Jerusalem were, as you will see, well covered by cartoonists both in Britain and in the United States. Despite the promise of a Jewish homeland made just weeks prior to the liberation of Jerusalem, the event was very much seen from a Christian perspective rather than a Jewish one. The majority of cartoonists depicted this as a continuation of the crusades from the Middle Ages, attempting to rid the Holy Land of the 'infidels'. Cartoons alongside editorials now showed this achievement in symbolic Christian terms. For instance, according to the *Philadelphia Evening Public Ledger*:

'Christian soldiers stand in possession of the ground in which the Cross was set up. At the darkest hour of the war, the capture of Jerusalem is a trumpet call to Christian civilisation to fight on until the Turko-Prussian foe, who would tear down the edifice of humanity which it has taken 2,000 years to build, is himself rendered harmless.'

This and similar editorials in other papers emphasised that Palestine had been liberated for Christian civilisation. General Allenby was seen as a modern-day Richard the Lionheart for having completed the unfinished crusade which his predecessors had failed to accomplish. No mention or reference was given to the Balfour Declaration. According to the *New York Evening Mail:*

'The taking of Jerusalem by the British marks a new epoch in the history of the holiest shrine of two great religions. It is also a dramatic illustration of the continuity of history. The task that baffled Richard Coeur de Lion in the twelfth century has been accomplished by General Allenby in the twentieth.'

It was not until Britain was granted a mandate for Palestine on 2 April 1920 at the San Remo Conference that the subject reappeared in cartoons. Even then it was invariably linked to Britain's other mandate in the Middle East: Mesopotamia (Iraq). At this juncture in time, Lloyd George's government was struggling with Britain's post-war economic downturn. Unemployment was rising while spending cuts were hitting the most vulnerable in society. With the state of Britain's finances in mind, many cartoonists, from around 1921, began to depict the overburdened British taxpayer as having to bear the full brunt of the financial outlay required to maintain the mandates.

Unsurprisingly, Palestinian Arabs were unhappy with the Balfour Declaration from the outset, despite the reassurances that it would safeguard their civil and religious rights. Increasing Arab opposition towards the mandate also failed to attract the attention of cartoonists. For instance, the Arab riots in Palestine that took place in 1920 and 1921 against the likelihood of a Jewish homeland did not feature in any cartoons in either Britain or the United States.

George E. Studdy, *Passing Show*
12 May 1917

By the mid-1920s, encouraged by the terms of the mandate, Jewish immigration into Palestine ran at a rate of almost 10,000 a year. This increased tensions, and swelled hostility from the Arab population. In the summer of 1929, Arab massacres of Jewish communities in Jerusalem, Hebron, Safed and Jaffa did prompt cartoonists to start covering the developing conflict between Jew and Arab in Palestine. From then on, until British forces left Palestine in 1948, poor old John Bull was regularly depicted as a beleaguered hapless policeman doing his best, trying to prevent Jew and Arab from harming each other. As exemplified by Strube's cartoon of 9 April 1930, (p.39) Prime Minister Ramsay MacDonald was struggling with a plethora of overseas commitments. From an imperialistic standpoint, many politicians at Westminster viewed the inhabitants of Palestine in what today would be considered a racist and condescending manner. Successive Colonial Secretaries such as Winston Churchill, Lord Passfield and Malcolm MacDonald thought they knew what was best for the indigenous population, believing them too primitive and childlike to run their own affairs. In a speech before an imperial conference in June 1921, Churchill had explained why the British were not granting Palestinian Arabs the benefits of self-rule, stating:

'There is no doubt that these turbulent peoples are apt to get extremely bored if they are subject to a higher form of justice and more efficient administration than those to which they have for centuries been accustomed. At any rate, we have reverted perforce, and by the teaching of experience, to more primitive methods.'

At the time India was viewed in similar terms in regard to ethnic conflict and 'natives' agitating for political rights. The then Conservative Party chairman, Leopold Amery, remarked how the violence in Palestine would be 'familiar to most Indian administrators'. Cartoonists seem to have been heavily influenced by such views and, as a consequence, depicted Jews and Arabs as squabbling children or innocents with consecutive British Colonial Secretaries trying their paternalistic and patronising best to keep the peace between the two warring factions.

The demand for Jewish immigration into Palestine might have settled down had Hitler not become German chancellor in early 1933. The Nazis quickly introduced legislation in Germany which made day-to-day life for Jewish people impossible. In the face of increasing legal oppression and physical violence, many Jews tried desperately to flee Germany. While American cartoonists focused on the Nazi repression of Jews, their British counterparts emphasised the desperate struggle fleeing Jewish refugees faced in finding countries that would take them. Among those refugees who were successful in escaping were

Jewish cartoonists Victor Weisz ('Vicky'), Joseph Flatter, Stephen Roth and Walter Trier. Vicky, who was born in Berlin in 1913, had joined the graphics department of the radical anti-Hitler journal *12 Uhr Blatt*, and by 1929 was sports and theatre cartoonist on the paper. He produced his first anti-Nazi cartoon that year, but in 1933 the paper was taken over by the Nazis and by 1935 Vicky had fled to London. Joseph Flatter left Austria for London in 1934. Despite his anti-Nazi stance, he was arrested and interned as an 'enemy alien' on the Isle of Wight when war broke out in 1939. Once released, he drew cartoons for the *Spectator* and at the Ministry of Defence. Among his work was *Mein Kampf*, which parodied Hitler's book by combining actual quotes from the text with mocking illustrations. Flatter wrote: 'I drew many hundreds of cartoons during the war and, to my surprise, ideas never failed me. The moving force was hatred, it took concrete shape before my eyes. And my hatred of those responsible for the wanton cruelty done to so many innocent victims was boundless. I went about in the shape of my adversaries. I crept into their skin. I drew, hanged and quartered them.' In 1931, Stephen Roth moved to Prague, where he drew sports cartoons, joke illustrations and portraits for various papers and magazines, signing his work 'Stephen'. In 1935, he became cartoonist on the anti-Nazi weekly *Demokraticky*. In 1938, he was forced to flee Czechoslovakia prior to the Nazi occupation. He settled in London and contributed political cartoons to the *Sunday Pictorial*. In 1936, Walter Trier escaped Germany with his family and settled in England.

Other cartoonists chose the United States as a refuge. Like Vicky, Eric Godal was born in Berlin, and in 1933 only narrowly escaped the Gestapo, who had come to arrest him. His cartoons criticising the Nazis had quickly made him a marked man. Godal caught wind of the arrest and hailed a taxi that took him to Czechoslovakia. In Prague, he worked with many other German Jewish refugees to publish an anti-fascist satirical magazine. He then fled to New York City, eventually replacing Theodore Geisel (Dr Seuss) as the political cartoonist for *P.M.*, a left-wing daily newspaper. His widowed mother, Mrs Anna Marien-Goldbaum, also attempted to flee Germany to join her son in New York, but travelled on the ill-fated cruise liner the S.S. *St. Louis*. The ship had set sail from Hamburg in May 1939, supposedly with visas to enter Cuba as a stopping point before those on board would be granted visas to enter the United States. Under pressure from the US and other quarters, the Cubans revoked the transit visas and the ship was denied entry to US ports. Two heartbreaking letters 'from an aged mother on the wandering steamship to her son, an artist, in New York' were published in the *New York Daily Mirror*. 'It is so strange how near and yet how much cut off we really are,' Mrs Goldbaum wrote. 'I feel that you are backing me from far away, and that gives me courage to go on.' She tried to put on a brave face: 'I still have the hope that President Roosevelt and other influential people will help us ... I shall not lose courage until the happy end is reached.' Unfortunately, she and the 936 other German Jewish refugees aboard the ship were sent back to Europe. She was later murdered by the Nazis. Arthur Szyk's mother would suffer the same fate as Godal's. She was gassed at the Chełmno extermination camp in Poland in 1942.

Szyk, who had fled Europe in 1937 and settled in New York in 1940, felt that all cartoonists should speak out against the Nazi tyranny: 'An artist, especially a Jewish artist, cannot be neutral in these times. He cannot escape to still lifes, abstractions, and experiments. Art that is purely cerebral is dead. Our life is involved in a terrible tragedy, and I am resolved to serve my people with all my art, with all my talent, with all my knowledge.' Living in Connecticut, Szyk drew for the *New York Post* and contributed a steady stream of anti-Nazi cartoons. He saw himself as 'Roosevelt's soldier with a pen' and wrote, 'I consider myself as being on duty in my cartoons.' The president's wife, Eleanor Roosevelt, once remarked, 'This is a personal war of Szyk against Hitler, and I do not think that Mr Szyk will lose this war!'

Szyk and Godal's devotion to the Allied war effort was matched by their growing concern for Jews stuck in Nazi-occupied Europe. In 1941, Szyk joined forces with the Bergson Group, a band of Jewish activists who lobbied the Roosevelt administration to rescue endangered Jews. After the war, the Bergsonites rallied American public support for the Jewish underground's revolt against the British in Palestine. Szyk's dramatic illustrations often featured in the full-page advertisements in American newspapers inciting violence against the perceived British occupiers. Many American cartoonists, Jewish and non-Jewish, supported opening the borders of Palestine to those fleeing from Europe. Britain's outright refusal to do so created much anti-British sentiment in the United States.

Nazi cartoonists revelled in Britain's troubles in Palestine in the late 1930s. Judging by their cartoons on the subject, the message was clear that Britain was using the Arabs and the Jews to bolster its own position in the Middle East. For instance, *Das Schwarze Korps* published a cartoon showing a British sergeant in colonial service uniform, splitting a piece of wood marked 'Palestine' with an axe. The cartoon is headed 'Divide and Rule'. The caption read: 'The British like dividing, but not with others'.

The Nazis, having dealt with dissent in their own country, did not appreciate criticism from abroad. In regard to the Nazi regime itself, all of

Britain's leading cartoonists were Germanophobic, many of whom, as already mentioned, had fought on the Western Front during the First World War. The *Daily Mail*'s Leslie Illingworth had once stood just metres away from the German dictator, and recalled: 'Hitler, in particular, seemed peculiarly repulsive, with his pasty, flabby face and a certain effeminacy about his movements.' Low and Strube lived in the vicinity of Golders Green, so they also understood perfectly how the Jewish community was adversely affected by the Nazis' persecution of the Jews in Germany. During the Berlin Olympics in 1936, Strube produced a cartoon to which Hitler himself took an instant dislike, resulting in all copies of that day's *Daily Express* being confiscated on arrival in Germany. A year later, Foreign Secretary Lord Halifax held talks with the Nazi Minister of Propaganda, Joseph Goebbels, who complained that British cartoonists were damaging Anglo-German relations. He explained that Hitler was extremely sensitive to criticism in the British press, especially from cartoonists. In 1939, an article in a German newspaper described the *Daily Mirror*'s Philip Zec, who was himself Jewish, as 'this filthy lying hyena scum'. According to Zec: 'The article went on to say that amongst the first dozen people to be shot when the Germans arrived in London would be me.' So it was of no surprise that every leading British cartoonist would end up in the Nazis' so-called Black Book. Had the Germans succeeded in invading Britain, then they would all have been put up against a wall and shot. Interestingly, only one American cartoonist's name was put in the Black Book: that of Jerry Doyle of the *Philadelphia Inquirer*. When the Nazis' Black Book was discovered after the war, nearly three thousand prominent Britons were mentioned in it. When David Low discovered his name was inside, he quipped: 'That is all right. I had them on my list too.'

In April 1945, with the grim, almost unbelievable discovery of the death camps, despite press announcements of mass atrocities having been reported throughout the war, cartoonists everywhere struggled to convey the enormity and depravity of the Nazis' genocide against European Jewry. For Jewish cartoonists it was even more of a dilemma. Apart from the disbelief and trauma they must personally have felt, they were conscious throughout the war not to make it all about the Jews. This was because antisemitic sentiments in both Britain and the United States, and encouraged by the Nazis themselves, falsely claimed that the Jews were the reason for the war in the first place; that they had caused it and/or were the reason for it being fought. There is not a single cartoon on the subject with even a single reference to Jews having been the greatest victims of these camps. Soviet cartoonist Boris Efimov, who became the world's oldest Jew in 2009 at 109 years old, was not allowed at any time during the war to mention Jewish suffering. The Soviet view was that everyone had suffered hardship and annihilation, not just the Jews. Efimov travelled with the writer Vasily Grossman to the death camps of Treblinka and Majdanek within days of them being liberated by Russian troops. According to Efimov: 'I will never forget the moment that I arrived at the death camps. As I was walking around, I came to a women's bunk. I don't know what pulled me there, but I went to one of the beds and put my hand under the mat, and happened to come across a holiday prayer book, the "*machzor* for Yom Kippur".' Boris gave the prayer book to his mother and said it was this one thing that reconnected him to Judaism for the rest of his life, although of course he had to keep this to himself.

With the end of the Second World War and the frightening reality that the Nazis had murdered almost six million of their brethren, Jews in Palestine used every method at their disposal to rid themselves of the war-weary British in order to create a Jewish state. Despite the heart-wrenching film-reel images of the Jewish refugee ships such as the *Haganah* shown in British cinemas, a campaign by Jewish terror groups in Palestine, for instance the Irgun and Stern Gang, which targeted British soldiers and policeman, only helped to alienate British and Australian cartoonists from their cause. As already mentioned, American cartoonists saw it quite differently, believing the Palestinian Jews

John Bull: Dear Creditors, I can't deny that both of you have just claims on the ground of certain promises made. In order not to wrong any of you, I propose to remain your trustee for ever.

The cartoonist believed that Britain's ultimate aim was to divide and rule in Palestine in order to hang on to its colonial possession.

Adam Shalin, *Behind the Barbed Wire: a Time to Cry and a Time to Laugh* (Palestine) 1946 were fighting British colonial attempts to retain their Empire.

Soon after Britain had handed the problem of Palestine over to the United Nations, there was a UN majority vote to divide the country into a Jewish and Arab state. This was accepted by the Jews but rejected by the Arab world. Soon after, surrounding Arab states attacked Jewish defence forces in Palestine. American cartoonists and those working for the *Communist Daily Worker* in Britain sided with the Jews against the Arabs. On 15 May 1948, the Jews declared independence with the creation of the state of Israel. A provisional government was set up, led by David Ben Gurion. Apart from the far left, most British cartoonists were simply pleased to see the back of Palestine, as it meant the safe return to these shores of beleaguered British troops, who had tried but failed to keep the peace between the warring factions.

David Low's private war against the Nazis, throughout the 1930s and 40s, especially his condemnation and ridicule of Hitler's persecution of the Jews, was in stark contrast to his views on the post-war situation in Palestine. Natural sympathy for Jewish refugees who had survived the Holocaust was undermined by the violent methods used by those in Palestine trying to bring about a Jewish state. According to Low:

'The state of Israel was achieved not in

Vicky Returns To His Studio

As we can see, Palestine remained one of the main topics in Britain for political cartoonists during the immediate post-war period.

Victor Weisz 'Vicky', *News Chronicle*
5 September 1947

peace and goodwill as had been hoped, but through a successful campaign of terrorism and assassination followed by war. Friends who had striven in the past for justice to the Jewish people were now uneasily doubtful whether complete justice had been done to the Arabs.'

On the principle that two wrongs never make a right, Low found abhorrent the fact that the Jewish refugee problem had only been resolved by the displacement of hundreds of thousands of Palestinian Arabs from their homes. Again, according to Low:

'Palestinian Arab refugees camped in miserable conditions over the frontier limit of the new state of Israel posed a formidable problem for international relief organisations to cope with.'

Low's view of what he saw as Israel's belligerence towards the surrounding Arab states, formed in the late 1940s, never changed. Low felt the new Israeli government should have come to terms with its Arab neighbours. Not surprisingly, his cartoons on the subject puzzled and infuriated many of his readers, both Jewish and non-Jewish. Letters of protest often appeared in the correspondence columns. 'Vicious', 'misleading' and 'mischievous' were some of the terms used to describe Low's anti-Israel stance. Low was criticised by Jewish readers for falling into the anti-Israel trap. 'He has,' said one reader, 'unmistakably expressed his one-sided and often unfair attitude towards the struggle for the establishment of the State

WHAT IS SOWN MUST COME UP

As seen in the cartoon above, Low was unable to understand Israel's belligerence towards the surrounding Arab states and therefore remained critical of the Jewish state for years after it had gained its independence. He felt that Israel should have tried to come to terms with its Arab neighbours rather than antagonise them.

David Low, *Manchester Guardian*
16 October 1956

of Israel.' In a letter to the editor of the *Manchester Guardian*, Labour MP K. Zilliacus wrote:

'Allow me as a non-Jewish reader to suggest that, after his cartoon on Israel, Low might rewrite and illustrate Aesop's fable about the wolf and lamb from the point of view of the wolf … The unpardonable offence of Israel, in the eyes of the Foreign Office, the State Department (and of Low?), is her refusal to be butchered to make an Arab Alliance.'

In later years, Low's cartoons criticising the new state were even discussed at a meeting of the Council of Manchester and Salford Jews, which was asked by several delegates to make a protest to the *Guardian*. At roughly the same time, a leader in the *Jewish Chronicle* said that it was 'pathetic to find such an old friend as Low in such a muddle about the whole issue'. However, the *Jewish Chronicle* emphasised that its criticism of Low in 'no way belittled his great achievement as an artist of universal regard belonging to the category of "our friends" who are always ready to defend the individual rights of Jews, wherever they may live'.

More than a hundred years on from the Balfour Declaration, its repercussions are still being felt today. The proverb 'the road to hell is paved with good intentions' seems perfectly apt in this instance, although Arthur Balfour could never have envisaged either the rise of Hitler or the horrors of the Holocaust and its impact on Palestine. The intent behind the 'Declaration' was no doubt naive and contradictory, but, in essence, was an honourable and well-meaning attempt to solve a 2,000-year-old imbroglio. In reality, setting out to create a Jewish homeland turned one set of people against another. The British tried to appease both sides, but soon fell intractably between two stools. The rise of Hitler and the threat of another world war led Britain to appease the surrounding Arab states by putting a stop to Jewish immigration at a time when it was desperately needed. To those escaping the Nazis it was a tragedy that, just before the outbreak of war, the 1939 British White Paper had severely restricted the immigration of Jews to Palestine. Whether justice was served in 1948 with the creation and then survival of the state of Israel, the cartoonists cannot tell us.

Do not forget that, unlike historians, cartoonists cannot offer the benefit of hindsight or rely on first-hand knowledge of the machinations of the main protagonists at the time. What the cartoonists have done is give us an acerbic and subjective commentary of what actually happened through their eyes in relation to Palestine and the Jews between 1917 and 1949. David Low once said the purpose of the cartoon was to amuse, inform and educate, and as such I cannot think of a more perfect medium for studying this tumultuous and unique period in modern history.

THE CARTOONS

A Great Incentive

Mehmed (reading despatch from the All-Highest): "'Defend Jerusalem at all costs for my sake. I was once there myself.'"

From Egypt, British forces were now on the verge of entering Palestine. On 27 October, the British artillery started a bombardment of Gaza. Newton Baker Jr, the American Secretary for War, had received reports that, 'under German supervision, a large number of fresh Turkish troops withdrawn from Mesopotamia and the Caucasus are being rushed to Palestine. It is believed that, in an attempt to regain their prestige, the Germans will afford whatever assistance is possible to the Turks in their effort to check the British taking Palestine.'

Leonard Raven Hill, *Punch*
14 November 1917

Too Bitter For His Taste

The Turks had been fed reports indicating that a third frontal attack on Gaza was imminent, but instead, on 31 October, an advance was launched on Beersheba, twenty miles south-east of Gaza. The lightly defended town fell to a daring British cavalry charge. The Turks then moved units to defend the area from the successful attack, weakening their own defences in Gaza.

George E Studdy, *Passing Show*
17 November 1917

The Bagdad Corridor

According to the *Newcastle Daily Chronicle*: 'The Turks are very much disturbed at the rapidity with which our troops are overrunning the Holy Land, and are anxiously asking whether they are to have any assistance from Germany. They would like the Kaiser to give a practical application to the promise he made in Damascus.'

John T. McCutcheon, *Chicago Tribune* (United States)
18 November 1917

John Bull:
'If I catch this turkey you may have a wing'

News of the Balfour Declaration reached the United States. However, only in the New York Jewish press was the story commented upon in political cartoons. Foshko by appearing to be suspicious of John Bull's intentions questions the veracity of the 'Declaration'.

Josef Foshko, *Der Tog* (United States)
22 November 1917

Pushing on in Palestine

As British forces encircled Jerusalem, the German public were being prepared for the fall of Jerusalem. *The Norddeutsche Allgemeine Zeitung* wrote: 'To cling to localities which would bring us no military advantage would be tantamount to a needless sacrifice of numerous Turkish forces, and our own troops would be bound to be involved in heavy losses. The only railway communication from Jerusalem – namely, the light railway – is no longer outside the enemy's reach.'

Clifford Berryman, *Washington Star* (United States)
26 November 1917

An Unthanks Giving Turkey

After Turkish troops had evacuated Jerusalem, officials of the Holy City prepared themselves to offer the keys to the city to the approaching British forces.

Fred Morgan, *Philadelphia Inquirer* (United States)
28 November 1917

Remember It, Mr Israel!

John Bull: 'Mr Israel, I'm giving you a secure home, but remember, you will have to move there!'

The Balfour Declaration, as it became known, was a letter sent on 2 November by the then Foreign Secretary, Arthur Balfour, to the Jewish community leader Lord Lionel Rothschild. The letter expressed the British government's support for 'the establishment in Palestine of a national home for the Jewish people'. The cartoonist implies that the Declaration also potentially jeopardised the national status of Jews around the world.

Cartoonist unknown, *Der Groyser Kundes (The Big Stick)* (United States)
30 November 1917

Home Once More

Many of the Jewish residents of the Old City of Jerusalem went out on the streets to cheer General Allenby as he entered it on 11 December. The British liberation of Jerusalem marked the physical salvation of the city's Jewish population, which was suffering from starvation, illness, squalor and death. This was the only cartoon in a British daily newspaper to feature Jerusalem from a Jewish perspective.

Joseph Morehead Staniforth 'JMS',
Western Mail
12 December 1917

Jerusalem 1917

On the day this cartoon was published, General Edmund Allenby took the surrender of Jerusalem. Allenby reportedly declared that 'the wars of the crusades are now complete'. In a deliberate contrast to the perceived arrogance and flamboyance of Kaiser Wilhelm's 1898 entry through Jerusalem on horseback, Allenby said: 'I won't ride my horse into the city into which my Lord rode a donkey.' Instead, Allenby entered the city on foot through the Jaffa Gate.

Charles Sykes, *Philadelphia Public Ledger* (United States)
11 December 1917

The Hour Of Deliverance

According to the *New York Evening Mail*: 'The taking of Jerusalem by the British marks a new epoch in the history of the holiest shrine of two great religions. It is also a dramatic illustration of the continuity of history. The task that baffled Richard Coeur de Lion in the twelfth century has been accomplished by General Allenby in the twentieth.'

Homer Stinson, *Daytona News* (United States)
12 December 1917

Another Capture

John Bull: 'Well done, old Lion heart. The Empire's proud of you.'

Prime Minister David Lloyd George heralded the capture of Jerusalem as 'a Christmas present for the British people.'

Joseph Morehead Staniforth 'JMS', *News of the World*
16 December 1917

After Seven Centuries

As we have seen the liberation of Jerusalem drew parallels both in the UK and the US with the crusades. *The Daily Herald* headline on the 11 December 1917 read: 'Jerusalem is rescued by the British after 673 years of Moslem rule / Great rejoicing in the Christian world / Jews everywhere in particular see the restoration of Palestine as part of Allies' programme.'

Daniel Fitzpatrick, *St. Louis Dispatch* (United States)
18 December 1917

The Last Crusade

Coeur-de-Lion (looking down on the Holy City): 'My dream come true!'

General Allenby was given the original of this cartoon by Ewan Agnew, son of *Punch*'s proprietor. Agnew had been Allenby's ADC and had followed him from the Western Front to Egypt, where he had fallen gravely ill and had to be invalided home.

Bernard Partridge, *Punch*
19 December 1917

The Outcasts

In November 1898, when visiting Damascus, Kaiser Wilhelm had ironically said: 'The three hundred million Mohammedans who live scattered over the globe may be assured of this, that the German Emperor will be their friend at all times.'

James Affleck Shepherd 'Jas', *The People*
23 December 1917

The Modern Crusader

American cartoonists appeared to be ignorant of British army battledress, and generally drew British 'Tommies' in the same manner they drew their own American troops.

Sid Chaplin, *St. Louis Republic* (United States)
11 January 1918

Pretty Cold Weather

Clifford Berryman, *Washington Star* (United States)
19 January 1918

Trapped. A Big Catch of Turkeys in the Far East

According to the *Western Mail*: 'Another great offensive has been started by the Allies – this time in Palestine where General Allenby has achieved a notable success. Our troops have broken right through the Turkish lines stretching from the Jordan to the Mediterranean, and advanced to a depth of nineteen miles on a sixteen-mile front, taking 3,000 prisoners. The Turks are in rapid retreat towards Shechem [modern-day Nablus] and it is considered they will have the greatest difficulty in extricating their forces. Our cavalry is in the rear of the retreating Turks, and another mounted division is advancing northwards with the object of cutting off the retreat towards El Atule and Beisan (the ancient Beth Shean) 36 miles from Haifa on the way to Damascus.'

Joseph Morehead Staniforth 'JMS',
Western Mail
24 September 1918

A Knock-Out

Joseph Morehead Staniforth 'JMS', *Western Mail*
30 September 1918

Palestine

Dutch cartoonist Louis Raemakers had fled to Britain during the First World War when the Kaiser, who despised the way Raemakers depicted him, put a bounty of 12,000 marks on the cartoonist's head.

Louis Raemaekers, *Western Mail*
30 September 1918

'Better join us, Sammy, there's a nice bit for you'

With the Exception of Armenia the Fate of Turkey is Practically Settled—

At the San Remo Peace Conference of Allied Powers in 1920, the French and the British took over former Ottoman territories Syria, Lebanon, Palestine, Jordan and Iraq, in the guise of League of Nations mandates. The Peace Conference also effectively gave the Greeks possession of Asia Minor and 'Ionia' (western Anatolia); the Italians got the Dodecanese Islands and a 'zone of influence' in south-western Anatolia. At the time, the United States was considering taking the mandate for Armenia.

William Charles Morris, *New York Tribune* (United States)
7 June 1919

The Return From The Crusade

Field-Marshal Allenby: 'Singing from Palestine hither I come; Lady-Love, Lady-Love, welcome me home.'
Britannia: 'I do indeed – with all my heart!'

According to the *Manchester Evening News*: 'Field Marshal Sir E. Allenby the conqueror of Palestine received a fitting welcome when he arrived at Dover and London yesterday. At each place he was cheered to the echo by enthusiastic crowds, and seemed to be almost overwhelmed by the people's enthusiasm.' In a speech to the welcoming crowds he said: 'This mission was wonderful. Jerusalem meant a lot to us all, as the holy place of Christian, Jew, and Mohamedan. All three faiths were represented in my army. Towards the close of the campaign two thirds of the troops under my command were Mohamedans, and there are no troops more loyal to the cause and to the Empire. It was this spirit of loyalty which made the cosmopolitan army so homogeneous.'

Bernard Partridge, *Punch*
17 September 1919

A conference took place in London, chaired by Prime Minister David Lloyd George, which discussed how to divide the territories of the old Ottoman Empire. This cartoon refers to the movement to create an independent Syrian state with authority over the area of Palestine. The cartoonist feared that the creation of such a state would result in similar or worse violence against the Jewish people in its territory. The standing figure is labelled 'Arabia' and holds a scroll reading 'Arab pogroms'. It references the Arab attack on the Jewish settlement at Matulla [modern-day Metula] in Palestine. At this time, Kamel el Husseini, Grand Mufti of Jerusalem, was protesting against the British pro-Zionist policy and declared that the Arabs would never allow the Zionists to take possession of their country: 'Our fate depends on the English people. We want to live in peace in our own country. We are poor, and few of us are educated. If the Jews come, with all their wealth, modern methods, and husbandry behind them, in 15 years our peasantry will have emigrated.'

Art Young, *Der Groyser Kundes* (The Big Stick) (United States)
19 March 1920

Jerusalem 1921

Sir Herbert Samuel: 'Hullo, Alf! What do you think of Jerusalem?'
Sir Alfred Mond: 'Top hole, Herb. But not much anno domini about it – what?'
Sir Herbert Samuel: 'No; more like a bit of "anno mondi".'

Sir Alfred Mond MP visited Palestine to confer with its High Commissioner, Sir Herbert Samuel, on the finances required to create a Jewish homeland there. Mond stated that, despite wartime neglect, when the most fertile districts had become desert, the possibilities for Palestine both as a producing and a consuming country were immense. 'The enthusiasm of the Jews for the reconstruction of their national home was unbounded,' Mond said, 'and Jews were walking from all over Europe to the Holy Land, their journeys sometimes taking as long as eleven months.'

W A Lloyd, *Punch*
19 Janurary 1921

Speaking Of Mandates

Unlike its wartime allies, the United States did not request or receive any mandated territories.

Edward Samuel 'Tige' Reynolds - *Portland Oregonian* (United States) 7 April 1921

Unpaying Guests

As Colonial Secretary, Winston Churchill was given special responsibility for Britain's mandates for Iraq and Palestine. Lloyd George told Churchill that it was of the utmost importance he reduce the administrative costs of governing these former parts of the Ottoman Empire. Churchill stated that the anti-government press had been endeavouring to suggest that the creation of a Middle East branch of the Colonial Office implied new burdens on the British taxpayer, but his intention was exactly the opposite. He hoped that with the help of the Arab government, supported by moderate military force, Britain might be able to do the job without imposing unjustifiable expense on the British taxpayer.

Leonard Raven Hill, *Punch*
13 April 1921

A Warning to East Hertfordshire To-Day

'Polling takes place in East Hertfordshire to-day. It is also Ascot Gold Cup Day. Our cartoonist uses the two events to point a moral. At the moment the Government is cutting off home subsidies only to put all the money on to Waste in Mesopotamia and Palestine. But the electors will not be deceived by this operation.'

As the British Government faced a post-war economic downturn, cartoonists became ever more fixated with the cost to the taxpayer of the Mandates in the Middle East.

William Haselden, *Daily Mirror*
16 June 1921

Going to a Hot Spot

The Black and Tans were a special unit of Britain's Royal Irish Constabulary, and known for committing some particularly heinous acts of violence and intimidation in Southern Ireland. After the Irish War of Independence, Winston Churchill re-assigned many of these men who comprised the Black and Tans to continue their campaign of terror in Palestine so as to quell Arab unrest over the Mandate. Churchill privately acknowledged that the Tans were 'a gang of murderers,' while also publicly declaring them a 'picked force of white gendarmerie' for the newly established British Mandate of Palestine.'

Cartoonist Unknown, *Graphic & Sphere* (Ireland)
21 January 1922

Uncorked by the War

The question is how to get him back into the vase.

Arab opposition to the British and French mandates in the Middle East was expressed through anti-Zionist riots. An Arab delegation of notables visited London to demand that the Balfour Declaration be repudiated. Instead they proposed the creation of a national government with a parliament democratically elected by the country's Muslims, Christians and Jews. Alarmed by the extent of Arab opposition, the British government issued a White Paper in June 1922 declaring that Great Britain did 'not contemplate that Palestine as a whole should be converted into a Jewish National Home, but that such a Home should be founded in Palestine'.

Cartoonist Unknown, *Daily Star*
(Montreal Canada)
3 June 1922

The Russian monopolist: 'We admit that maintenance of the tree is expensive but look what wonderful fruit it produces.'

Pincus Rutenberg was a former Russian revolutionary who fled to Palestine in 1919. He is best known for establishing the electrification of Palestine, having secured the finance from the British government. According to the *Sunday Mirror*: 'The way Mr. Rutenberg strolled into Palestine and got out of Sir Herbert Samuel a million-pound concession for harnessing the Jordan has left everybody gasping. Rutenberg is a Russian Jew who was Kerensky's head policeman in Petrograd. He is said to be "very enthusiastic" and to be ordering his machinery in Germany. Wouldn't you be enthusiastic if you could pick up big concessions on the beach while the simple British taxpayer pays for an army to protect your works?'

Percy Fearon 'Poy', *Daily Mail*
7 May 1922

The Half-Promised Land

Bernard Partridge, *Punch*
7 June 1922

The Last of the Crusaders

(After Tenniel's 'White Knight' in *Through the Looking Glass*) Mr Winston Churchill and Sir Alfred Mond.

Winston Churchill, depicted as the white knight, assists Alice, here in the guise of Sir Alfred Mond, in the fulfilment of her dream of a Jewish homeland. According to the *Sunday Mirror*: 'Sir Alfred Mond's audacious defence of the Coalition's mad and wildly extravagant policy of creating a "national home" for the Jews in Palestine at the expense of the British taxpayer leaves me gasping. The handful of Zionists in Palestine would be swept headlong in a day if they were not backed by British baronets. The Zionists in this country cannot have it both ways, and if they want to make Palestine their national home, they must surrender their British citizenship.'

W A Lloyd, *Punch*
12 July 1922

'I wonder how many houses could be built with all that money?'

The resounding promise of the Lloyd George coalition after the armistice was to make Britain a land 'fit for heroes to live in'. Yet by 1922 more than 1.5 million of the adult population were unemployed. Furthermore, housing facilities fell woefully short of Lloyd George's rhetoric of 'habitations for heroes'.

Sidney Strube, *Daily Express*
4 September 1922

The Devil's Jumps

The Forestry Commissioners threaten the Devil's Jumps in Surrey; if Lord Curzon has his way, the Devil's Jumps in the Near East will go on for ever.

Press Lords such as Northcliffe, Rothermere and Beaverbrook used their newspapers to continually criticise and highlight to the British taxpayer the huge cost of maintaining the mandates in Palestine and Mesopotamia.

Sidney Strube, *Daily Express*
1 March 1923

Mum-mies the Word!

There is something about sealing things up for 3,000 years that appeals to me.

On 16 February, English archaeologist Howard Carter discovered the sealed burial chamber of the ancient Egyptian ruler King Tutankhamen in Thebes, Egypt. 'Mum's the word' means to keep silent or quiet. In other words, Palestine, Mesopotamia, income tax and war were considered by the cartoonist to be unpalatable to the British people and metaphorically should be buried and forgotten about.

Bruce Bairnsfather, *The Bystander*
14 March 1923

An Everyday Knock-out

The big boxing match between Battling Siki and McTigue takes place in Dublin to-day.

Sidney Strube, *Daily Express*
17 March 1923

Dear Marriages.

Another dress allowance case.

The son of Lord Rothermere, Esmond Harmsworth MP, addressed 400 members of the Thanet Conservative Association, where he stated: 'The Near East has always been the womb of future wars. We should clear out of Mesopotamia and Palestine. Millions of the taxpayers' money are being wasted there. The people do not want us. We are only keeping there by aeroplanes and bayonets. As soon as those are withdrawn the two lands will go back to their natural rulers. These places, already, are bleeding the taxpayers white. They will foment future wars. They add no glory to our Flag. Let the country decide to quit them.'

Pearcy Fearon 'Poy', *Weekly Dispatch*
18 March 1923

'...But Few Are "Chosen"'

I have always thought that for a National Home for Jews, the biggest expense would be incurred in getting the first one to go there.

Despite the country advocating Palestine as a Jewish homeland, very few British Jews took up the offer. Under-Secretary for the Colonies William Ormsby-Gore suggested this as the reason: 'I hardly think any Jew would select Palestine as a country to which to emigrate unless he had some religious convictions, though he may not be strictly orthodox.'

Bruce Bairnsfather, *The Bystander*
21 March 1923

British Hawk (half-starved): 'I wonder how those carrion would like to "carry on" with the little bit I get!'

According to the *Sunday Mirror*: 'In Palestine the Government are paying indirectly the most enormous agricultural subsidy in the world. They are spending at the rate of £20 per head yearly upon 79,000 Jews, many of them Bolshevists from Eastern Europe, to provide them with the protection of armoured cars and aircraft while they are taught to till the soil. Twenty pounds a head for Palestine Jews but nothing for Norfolk or Shropshire! Money for Arabs, money for Palestine Jews, but not a shilling for British agriculture!' At this time, Prime Minister Andrew Bonar Law oversaw major cuts to the Royal Air Force's budget.

Leo Cheney, *Passing Show*
7 April 1923

When Arab folk resent our joke
And all their posts resign,
It's clear that they don't mean to play
The 'pal' in Palestine.

Sir Herbert Samuel, who served as High Commissioner in Palestine from 1920 to 1925, was the first Jewish ruler to exercise authority in the Holy Land since the collapse of Shimon bar Kokhba's revolt against Rome in the year 135. There was little political cooperation between Arabs and Jews in Palestine. Samuel tried to win Arab cooperation with offers first of a legislative council that would reflect the Arab majority and then of an Arab agency. Both offers were rejected by the Arabs as falling far short of their national demands. Nor did the Arabs wish to legitimise a situation they rejected in principle.

Frank Holland, *John Bull*
30 June 1923

Arthur Coeur-de-Zion

Lord Balfour: 'I'll sing thee songs of Araby, and tales of fair Judaea.'

On 1 April, Arthur Balfour visited Palestine for the first time. The occasion was the official opening of the Hebrew University of Jerusalem. Palestinian Jews were delighted he had made the journey, but Arab shops closed in protest. Later, driving on to Damascus, Balfour was met by 6,000 Arabs demonstrating outside his hotel. Upon his return to England, he was asked about the events in Damascus and said: 'I have been in no way disturbed by what happened in Damascus. Nor have I altered my views. I am more sanguine than ever about the future of Zionism. I think it is being approached in the right way and the Jews are fully conscious of the necessity of working harmoniously with the Arabs. In fact, it is coming and would be there now if agitators would leave things alone.`

Bernard Partridge, *Punch*
8 April 1925

WAILS OR WARWHOOPS?

Deadly riots engulfed Palestine in August 1929, marking a turning point in Arab–Jewish relations in the country. Erupting in Jerusalem, they quickly spread to Hebron and Safad. The violence took place in the context of rising Arab frustration over the increase in Jewish immigration and Zionist land purchases. The immediate trigger, however, was access to and custody of the Wailing Wall and Temple Mount in Jerusalem, where the Jews had been challenging Muslim control since the beginning of the mandate. More than 200 deaths occurred in four days of violent clashes between 23 and 26 August.

David Low, *Evening Standard*
27 August 1929

His Hands Full

John Bull: And they call this the holiday month!

The minority Labour government, already beset with domestic woes and foreign entanglements, felt it had no choice but to establish a commission of inquiry so as to investigate the unprecedented violence taking place in Palestine between Jews and Arabs.

Walter Holt, *Western Mail*
28 August 1929

When a Local Mandate Becomes Everybody's Business

From 23 to 24 August, more than sixty Jews were murdered in what became known as the Hebron Massacre. It would go down as one of the bloodiest slaughters of Jewish civilians during the period of the Palestine mandate. Hebron is an ancient city and the resting place of many biblical patriarchs and matriarchs. Jews had been living peacefully in Hebron among their Muslim and Christian neighbours for hundreds of years prior to the massacre.

J.N. 'Ding' Darling,
The Des Moines Register (United States)
29 August 1929

The Palestine Mandate

Britannia: 'They gave me the scales of justice and her sword. I have used the scales; I had hoped not to have to use the sword.'

The cartoon is responding to the Arab massacres of Jewish communities in Jerusalem, Hebron, Safed and Jaffa. The Arab newspaper *al-Hayat* said that, in one stroke, the British had destroyed Arab confidence in the British. For the Zionists not to have the Passfield White Paper implemented was crucial. However, the subsequent nine years saw an unprecedented increase in the number of Jews and their proportion of the population. Arab anger against Zionism continued to grow at the same time.

Bernard Partridge, *Punch*
4 September 1929

WHEN the big war ended, Britain took the mandate for Palestine. France and Italy took other mandates. Thus they made themselves responsible for obtaining peace and order in various parts of Europe that don't belong to them.

That was a good thing, as now appears with the Arabs breaking out murderously in Palestine.

In that Palestine affair Uncle Sam sympathetically watches John Bull going against the Arabs. He hopes that Britain will carry out the solemn undertaking. But there are so many Americans in Jerusalem, some of them murdered, that this country would be glad to take a hand in making it clear that murders can't go unpunished.

However, Uncle Sam and the average American is glad that when the mandates are distributed, and the mandate for Turkey picked out for Uncle Sam, the latter, most mysteriously, had brains enough to decline it

Many are the millions of Turks, all Mohammedans, all fighters—better fighters two to one than those Arabs of Palestine.

It would have been pleasant to learn suddenly that it was part of our duty to go over there and pacify the whole of Turkey.

Our patriots would need many billions of dollars to get started on that.

A Real Man's Job

Despite having been offered Turkey, the United States refused to accept any League of Nations mandates and was, as a result, 'popular and respected throughout the Middle East'. Indeed, Americans were seen by the Arabs as good people, untainted by the selfishness and duplicity associated with Europeans.

T. E. Powers, *San Francisco Examiner* (United States)
7 September 1929

Squally Weather!

John Citizen (to Lord Passfield, Colonial Secretary): 'Good Heavens! ... What on earth are you going to do with them?'

'The report of the Commission of Inquiry into the Palestine riots, in which Jews were massacred by Arabs, is expected to prove sensational. The population is overwhelmingly Arabic and is fanatically hostile to Jewish immigration, which is taking place under our rule.'

Wallace Coop 'Wal', *News of the World*
16 March 1930

To-Day's Breathless Interview

Despite the violence and unrest, Prime Minister Ramsay MacDonald insisted that Britain would continue to administer Palestine in accordance with the terms of the mandate as approved by the Council of the League of Nations.

Sidney Strube, *Daily Express*
9 April 1930

The Innocence of Arthur

League of Nations (courteously): 'So you won't want this pail of whitewash after all?' Mr Henderson: 'Very kind of you to say so. The lily, of course needs no painting.'

Foreign Secretary Arthur Henderson was in Geneva to receive the report by the Council of the League of Nations on the riots that had taken place in Palestine. The report contained little criticism of the British government, which it felt had restored and maintained order, and acquitted it of any charge of failure in its duties with regard to the mandate. A relieved Henderson said that the British government would seek to promote goodwill between Arabs and Jews, without which they recognised that peace and prosperity in Palestine could not be secured. After speeches by several members of the Council, general confidence in the mandatory power was expressed.

Bernard Partridge, *Punch*
17 September 1930

Solomon Passfield

Solomon (throwing the £2,500,000 loan): 'Come, come, ladies, never mind the baby. Here's something worth quarrelling about.'

The Passfield White Paper, issued on 20 October by Colonial Secretary Lord Passfield, called for restrictions on Jewish immigration to Palestine in order to contain the conflict between the Arabs and the Jews. As a sweetener, he proposed a loan of £2,500,000 for agricultural development to be enjoyed by both Arab and Jewish communities. The strategy failed as Arabs felt that the British were not keeping to agreed Jewish quotas, as well as appearing to do little to stop illegal landings. Conversely, Jews felt that the restrictions imposed on them went against the principles of the Balfour Declaration.

Sidney Strube, *Daily Express*
20 November 1930

All Fools' Day in Germany

Chancellor Hitler: 'As a retaliation for the false statement by foreigners that we have been persecuting the Jews, I forbid you to enter this shop.'

Less than three months after coming to power in Germany, Adolf Hitler permitted an organised boycott of Jewish businesses while beginning to exclude Jews from public life. The boycott was presented to the German people as an act of revenge for German and foreign Jews spreading 'atrocity stories' to damage Germany's reputation.

Bernard Partridge, *Punch*
5 March 1933

Relativity

After learning that Nazi stormtroopers had broken into his Berlin apartment and country home, Einstein fled to Belgium. There he renounced his German citizenship and sent off his resignation from the Prussian Academy of Science. On 2 April his Berlin bank account and apartment were seized. Einstein spent the next six months in Belgium, Switzerland and England, weighing up his options and rethinking his commitment to pacifism. Together with Sigmund Freud he published 'Why War?' and in a major speech at the Royal Albert Hall he called on Europeans to fight fascism in order to save civilisation.

Edmund Duffy, *Baltimore Sun*
(United States)
31 March 1933

German 'Gifts' to the Nation

William Beveridge, director of the London School of Economics, started a rescue effort to save Jews fleeing Nazi oppression after reading in March 1933 of the dismissal of Jewish scientists and other professionals in Germany. Outraged, he and some of his prominent colleagues founded what became known as the Society for the Protection of Science and Learning. Most of those rescued had already achieved distinction in academia or the arts. Of the 2,600 rescued, twenty became Nobel laureates, fifty-four were elected Fellows of the Royal Society, thirty-four became Fellows of the British Academy, and ten received knighthoods.

Carl Rose, *Jewish Daily Bulletin*
(United States)
30 April 1933

On the Altars of the Nazis

On 10 May, Joseph Goebbels, Nazi Germany's Minister of Propaganda, led a book-burning event near the Berlin Opera House. Goebbels declared the event 'the end of Jewish intellectualism'. The burned books were written by more than 200 authors, scientists, philosophers, artists and journalists. Of these, two-thirds were Jewish. In total, 100 million books were burned between 1933 and 1945 in territories occupied by Nazi Germany. In 1821, German Jewish writer Heinrich Heine had prophetically said: 'Where they burn books, they will ultimately burn people too.'

Jacob Burck, *Daily Worker* (United States)
11 May 1933

As It Was in the Beginning

According to the cartoonist: 'They burned the books in Germany during a soft spring drizzle on a May evening in 1933. There was nothing casual about this symptomatic assault upon the free mind of man. The fires rose in the public squares of thirty university towns in the same hour. Youngsters from the universities, impassioned, intent, blind-piled their armloads on the pyres ... They burned Thomas Mann and Freud and Emil Ludwig, and the novelist Remarque, and graceful, penetrative Schnitzler, and Wassermann and the Zweigs and the poet Franz Werfel.'

Jerry Doyle, *Philadelphia Inquirer* (United States)
15 November 1933

'We're doing nothing to prevent him from entering the Olympics.'

The Nazis began to exclude Jews from German sport and recreational facilities. Barred from German sports clubs, Jewish athletes flocked to separate Jewish associations, but their facilities were no match for those of the well-funded German group.

Carl Rose, *Jewish Daily Bulletin* (United States)
26 November 1933

The Largest Purveyors of Their Line in the World

Both Julius Streicher and Joseph Goebbels founded violently antisemitic newspapers, *Der Stürmer* and *Der Angriff* respectively. Their aim was to demonise Jews and to create a climate of hostility and indifference towards their plight.

Carl Rose, *Jewish Daily Bulletin*
(United States)
13 June 1934

Der Boomerang

Dr. Schacht, President of the Reichsbank and Minister for Trade, in a recent speech said that the persecution of the Jews was detrimental to German trade.

Hitler rejected an appeal made to him by Dr Schacht to put the brakes on anti-Jewish agitation in Germany. He had protested at the placing of unnecessary obstacles in the way of his economy schemes while stressing the dangers of political and economic repercussions abroad as a result of the campaign. Schacht feared an extension of the boycott of German goods in America, and predicted incidents similar to the tearing down of the swastika flag on the S.S. *Bremen* in New York.

Sidney Strube, *Daily Express*
9 August 1935

Out of the House of Bondage

'Mr. McDonald, an American, resigning as High Commissioner for Refugees from Germany, says that over a half million people against whom no charge can be made except that they are not "Nordic" – not only Jews, but "non-Aryan" Christians, who are treated as Jews – are being crushed.'
'Vell, United Schtates, I don'd see any Moses among dem.'
'But there might be another Monash or another Reading.'

This cartoon was inspired by James J. McDonald's outspoken comments on the German Jewish situation. The year before, McDonald had resigned his post as League of Nations High Commissioner for Refugees from Germany and had demanded that the League intervene in Germany. Sir John Monash and Fanny Reading MBE were distinguished Jewish Australians.

Norman Lindsay, *Sydney Bulletin*
(Australia)
8 January 1936

'Come clean, Jew – you've been saving the lives of Aryans!'
The death rate in undernourished Germany has increased – but the Nazi ban on Jewish doctors continues.

In Germany the death rate had jumped considerably due to the dismissal of Jewish doctors, which unfavourably affected the level of efficiency in many hospitals. The total number of deaths in German cities with a population of 100,000 and above rose from 207,539 in 1934 to 221,631 in 1935, an increase of approximately eight per cent.

Will Dyson, *Daily Herald*
27 February 1936

Academic Instruction in Full Swing

Academic instructor: 'Hup! Two! Hup! Two!'
Students: 'Let's thrust a knife into a Jew's throat!!!'

One of the first objectives realised by the Nazis was the 'cleansing' of the German universities of their Jewish students and lecturers. This purge was connected with the attempt to 'coordinate' German academic life with the tenets of National Socialism. The National Socialist German Student League directly targeted Jewish students and any remaining Jewish faculty members.

Boris Efimov, *Izvestia* (Soviet Union)
23 April 1936

In Palestine now: 'A Policeman's lot is not a happy one.'

In April 1936, the Arabs launched a countrywide revolt against British rule in Palestine and the official policy of support for Jewish immigration to the country. Although Palestinians had engaged in organised resistance against British rule before 1936, this revolt was widespread, highly organised and sustained. Arab fighters from outside Palestine had also joined the struggle. The British army employed brutal measures to crush the revolt, including mass arrests, house demolitions and executions. An Arab attack on a Jewish bus on 15 April 1936 that killed three Jews led to a series of incidents that escalated into a major Arab revolt. An Arab Higher Committee, a loose coalition of Arab political parties, declared a six-month national strike in support of three basic demands: cessation of Jewish immigration, an end to all further land sales to the Jews, and the establishment of an Arab national government.

Bob Rodger, *Daily Record*
16 June 1936

JUMPED ON, WERE YOU? WOULD YOU LIKE US TO MAKE YOU A NICE CUP OF TEA ON THE HOME SECRETARY?"

Oswald Mosley led Britain's virulently antisemitic fascist movement, whose street fighters, known as Blackshirts, were notorious for their violence against Jews and left-wing opponents. During a debate in the House of Commons, after a Labour MP described how a young Jewish man and a woman walking together had been violently assaulted by 'nine black-shirted ruffians', the then Home Secretary, Sir John Simon, said: 'It made my blood boil. It was horrifying.' Simon also faced accusations that the police had been less than impartial when it came to the actions of Mosley's Blackshirts.

David Low, *Evening Standard*
13 July 1936

Order First: Or, The Problem of Palestine

Arab: 'Where do I come in?'
British Tommy: 'We'll see about that, mate; but this is where I do.'

Twenty thousand British troops were deployed to Palestine in order to forcibly put down the Arab revolt.

Ernest H. Shepard, *Punch*
7 October 1936

First Crusader: 'Alas, I failed to reach the Holy Land.'
Second ditto: 'Alas, old man, I didn't!'

The British government sent the Peel Commission to Palestine as a response to the Great Arab Rebellion that had broken out in April 1936. The Peel Commission report was published on 7 July. It recommended the partition of Palestine into two states, one Jewish and one Arab. This was the first time that a British political body had officially endorsed the idea of a Jewish state in Palestine rather than the more limited idea of a Jewish national homeland. The report also recommended that more than 200,000 Palestinians be transferred from their homes to accommodate the new Jewish state.

Will Dyson, *Daily Herald*
9 July 1937

THE JUDGEMENT OF SOLOMON CHAMBERLAIN

The biblical reference to Solomon was popular with cartoonists to show that the rivalry of Jews and Arabs in Palestine would help neither side gain what they wanted. In the Bible, Solomon had been required to decide which of two women was the mother of a baby, when each of them claimed parenthood. Both had recently given birth, but one child had died. Solomon announced that the child should be cut in two, so that each mother should have half. The real mother, unable to bear her son being killed, immediately offered it to the other woman, to save the child's life, whereas the other agreed to the proposal. The false mother was thus exposed, and Solomon returned the living child to its real mother.

David Low, *Evening Standard*
9 July 1937

Their Only Hope

Upon release of the Peel Commission report, the Zionist leadership was divided about how to react, and agreed to approve the principle of partition but not the specifics of the Peel partition map. The Palestinian leaders were outraged at the report and condemned the partition recommendation. They were firmly committed to setting up an independent Palestinian state in all of Palestine and were not prepared to give away the most fertile areas of that state to what they saw as European colonisers.

Wyndham Robinson, *Morning Post*
22 July 1937

The camel: 'Another blinkin' mirage!'

The Commons debate on the Palestine Report was described in the *Palestine Post* as the 'funeral of the Mandate'. The paper deplored the fact that the mandate, which was hailed fifteen years previously as one of the few positive results of the war, had now been torn up. It concluded by stating that 'through the mist of uncertainty a distant peak of hope can be discerned – that the Jews will unite with the Arabs'.

Will Dyson, *Daily Herald*
23 July 1937

STANDING ROOM ONLY.

As the persecution of Jews in Germany increased, growing numbers looked to Palestine. As already mentioned, the Peel Commission had recommended the partitioning of Palestine. Zionist critics objected to the restrictions on immigration and held that the proposed Jewish area was too small. The British Colonial Secretary, William Ormsby-Gore, contended that at least it established a Jewish state.

David Low, *Evening Standard*
30 July 1937

Roma Khayyám or The Arab and His Set

'And thou beside me booming in the wilderness.'

On 4 January, the BBC began short-wave broadcasting in Arabic, its first regular international service in a language other than English. This was to counter Italian propaganda put out by Italy's Arabic-language broadcasts. In the House of Commons, Foreign Secretary Anthony Eden warned the Italian government that its continued hostile propaganda in Palestine was making it more difficult for Great Britain and Italy to arrive at a mutual understanding.

Bernard Partridge, *Punch*
5 January 1938

Inferiority Complex

On 22 March, ten days after German troops had entered Austria, the Gestapo raided Sigmund Freud's apartment. His daughter Anna Freud was arrested and taken to the Gestapo headquarters, only returning after hours of questioning. The American ambassador to France, William C. Bullitt, a former patient of Freud's, sent the American Consul General John Wiley to Vienna to set in motion Freud's safe departure. A week later, Freud and his family gained permission to leave for England. Upon arriving in England, Sigmund wrote to cartoonist David Low: 'A Jewish refugee from Vienna, a very old man personally unknown to you, cannot resist the impulse to tell you how much he admires your glorious art and your inexorable, unfailing criticism.'

Edmund Duffy, *Baltimore Sun* (United States) 27 March 1938

The Beacon Light in the Midst of the World Storm

The United Palestine Fund appeal is to help the ship on its way to the only haven of rest for the Jew in the whole world today. '... and Jacob shall return, and shall be at rest and be secure, with none to terrify him.'

Jeremiah xxx

A national conference of the United Palestine Appeal in Chicago put forward a plan for the settlement of 500,000 Jewish refugees in Palestine over five years. Execution of the plan was contingent on fulfilment of 'the letter and spirit of the Palestine Mandate'.

Arthur Racey, *Montreal Daily Star* (Canada)
2 April 1938

Shakedown

The German government created financial difficulties for itself by funding an armament programme with promissory notes it could not pay back. On 26 April, the government issued an edict requiring Jews to declare their personal assets and authorising Hermann Goering to incorporate the money into the German economy. If they hid any assets, the Jews would receive an automatic ten-year prison term and have their wealth confiscated. With the military budget still growing, however, deficits worsened and Goering then introduced a law nationalising all property owned by German Jews.

Bruce Russell, *Los Angeles Times*
(United States)
29 April 1938

Simplified Finance

Herbert Block 'Herblock', *NEA Syndication*
(United States)
30 April 1938

As Ye Sow

According to the cartoonist: 'Hitler's Third Reich stepped on everybody's rights. First the Jews came under attack. Many were robbed, beaten and excluded from public service, the universities and the professions. Later came the dreaded concentration camps, where millions were exterminated.'

Ross A. Lewis, *Milwaukee Journal*
(United States)
2 June 1938

Whither?

When Hitler annexed Austria into the Third Reich, 185,000 Austrian Jews feared they would suffer the same treatment at the hands of the Nazis as German Jews. The sudden flood of emigrants created a major refugee crisis. President Roosevelt convened a conference in Evian, France. Despite the participation of delegates from thirty-two countries, including the United States, Great Britain, France, Canada and Australia, no permanent or comprehensive solution to the refugee crisis was found.

Sidney Strube, *Daily Express*
20 June 1938

They Know Well What They Do

An anti-Jewish speech by Joseph Goebbels announced that severe measures would be taken soon to suppress all Jewish businesses. This was followed by fresh press outbursts against the Jews, whose presence in the streets and cafes the newspapers described as 'scandalous impudence'. According to the *Daily Worker:* 'There was a renewed outbreak of Nazi terrorism against the Jews this weekend. Jewish shops were smashed up last night. Jewish workers arrested in hordes. All over Berlin many Jews remained in their homes to avoid molestation if not arrest, in streets, cafes and cinemas.'

Jimmy Friell 'Gabriel', *Daily Worker*
21 June 1938

A proposal that a committee be sent to Madagascar to investigate the possibility of establishing a Jewish colony there was met with strong opposition in American Jewish circles. Zionists opposed any development that did not feature Palestine, while non-Zionists were against any plan that would impose forced immigration on them. Many felt that Madagascar was inhospitable to Europeans and that there was a serious danger of potential settlers contracting endemic tropical diseases. The island of Madagascar was also discussed within the Nazi regime, which generally considered mass emigration at the time to be the 'Final Solution' to the Jewish problem.

David Low, *Evening Standard*
6 July 1938

Waiting

Although thirty-two countries attended the Evian Conference, President Roosevelt had chosen to intrude into a situation in which he was virtually powerless to act, bound as he was by highly restrictive American immigration laws. The conference was limited in the end to nothing more than humanitarian appeals.

Cecil Orr, *Daily Record*
9 July 1938

The New Moses and The Tables of the Law

According to the *Rugby Advertiser*: 'Shylock's famous speech, beginning "Hath not a Jew eyes" was quoted by the Rector of Rugby in a sermon on the persecution of the Jews in Germany and Austria. The Rector said that one result of the inclusion of Austria into the German State was that the sufferings of the Jews had been extended in a very intense form to Austria. The Archbishop of Canterbury had described the treatment of the Jews as devilish. Penalties were imposed upon them, and laws enacted against them, simply because they were Jews. They endured every kind of ignominy and insult, the violence used against them was almost incredible, all their goods were confiscated, and they were left penniless. During the last five years a quarter of the total Jewish population had been driven out of the country. A Nazi official had said, "We don't care what happens to them as long as we get rid of them."'

Aubrey Aria, *Daily Sun* (Australia)
16 July 1938

PALESTINE-LONDON SHUTTLE SERVICE.

Secretary of State for the Colonies Malcolm MacDonald told Parliament that the Woodhead Commission had almost completed taking evidence in Palestine. Due to the irreconcilable positions between Arabs and Jews over the Peel Commission partition plan for Palestine, the new commission under Sir John Woodhead had been instructed to gather evidence from the various parties and to recommend boundaries for two self-sufficient states, one Arab and one Jewish, to replace the British mandate.

David Low, *Evening Standard*
22 July 1938

The 'Moving' Finger Writes Again

Foreign Jews residing in Italy were given notice to quit in a drastic decree issued by the Italian government. This decree ordained that 'all foreign Jews who took up residence in Italy, Libya and the Dodecanese Islands after 1 January 1919 must leave these territories in six months'. All Italian citizenships granted to Jews since 1 January 1919 were to be revoked. Any Jews in the category prescribed by the decree who failed to leave by the end of six months were to be compulsorily expelled. A British United Press correspondent standing at a corner of the Piazza di Spagna saw a man who appeared to be a German Jew buy a paper and quickly read the decree. Then he turned to his companion with tears in his eyes and said in German: 'They've done it. I wouldn't have believed it.'

Will Mahony, *Sydney Daily News* (Australia)
28 July 1938

Good Clean Fun!

Following in the footsteps of Hitler, Mussolini initiated a persecuting crusade against the Jews in Italy. The Pope denounced these actions as 'unchristian' and 'inhuman' and stated that Italy had simply copied Germany in initiating a drive against the Jews. On hearing of this, Mussolini replied: 'You must know and let everyone know that in the racial question we shall go straight ahead. To say that fascism has imitated anyone is absurd.'

Bob Rodger, *Daily Record*
8 August 1938

The Riddle of the Sphinx

Malcolm MacDonald paid a surprise visit to Palestine. Without any officials to accompany him he set out on an RAF flying boat. He had interviews with the High Commissioner and others in charge of the country, walked around Jerusalem, and then travelled on to Egypt.

Harold Hodges, *Western Mail*
9 August 1938

He speaks for himself – positively no deception.

Further restrictions were imposed on the Jews in Italy after the Cabinet Council issued a decree prohibiting them from taking any part in state education. Persons of the Jewish race were not to be admitted in the role of teacher in state schools, nor in private schools whose syllabus and programme were legally recognised. Jews could not be admitted as university teachers, nor could they qualify for the title of 'independent teachers'.

Bob Rodger, *Daily Record*
5 September 1938

The New Cloak

According to the *Hastings and St Leonards Observer*: 'Mussolini turned round and asked the Jews whether they would not prefer the mandate of Palestine to be transferred from England to Italy, and the response of the Jews was thank you very much, we appreciate your kindness, but we prefer England. When Mussolini found the Jews would not support his desire for the transfer of Palestine from England to Italy, he immediately closed down all the facilities he had made for the Jews and declared himself Protector of Islam and began to woo the Arabs, and from that moment in 1931, trouble broke out in Palestine.'

Jimmy Friell 'Gabriel', *Daily Worker*
6 September 1938

SPECIAL PERFORMANCE FOR THE ARABS

Mussolini declared himself an opponent of the proposed Jewish state in Palestine, in order to curry favour with the Arabs and give encouragement to the ongoing Arab revolt in Palestine. On his self-proclaimed triumphal tour of Italy's North African possessions, the year before, he had proclaimed himself the 'Protector of Islam' after receiving the Sword of Islam during a lavish ceremony.

David Low, *Evening Standard*
7 September 1938

The Wondering Jews

Journalist for *Reynolds News*, Bernard Boothroyd 'Yaffles', was bemused by Hitler and Mussolini's attempts to rid themselves of their respective Jewish populations. In an article entitled 'The Wondering Jews' he wrote: 'It appears that the German and Italian Jews must leave the country they are in, yet may not enter any other. This raises difficult problems, largely mathematical. As geography is at present arranged, you cannot, while remaining on dry land, go out of one country without finding yourself immediately in another. You cannot stay in between, for a boundary line, though having plenty of length, has no breadth – a political difficulty which Euclid, whose logic was well in advance of his usefulness, did not foresee – and it has been found on examination that all Jews possess at least three dimensions. The Jews may neither move nor remain where they are.'

Carl Giles, *Reynolds News*
11 September 1938

Inconsistent

The quotation in Hitler's speech bubble comes from a speech delivered by him to a Nazi Party congress on 12 September. Hitler complained about the alleged persecution of Sudeten Germans, while at the same time persecuting German Jews.

George White, *Tampa Tribune*
(United States)
18 September 1938

European Cross Roads

European countries, including Poland, closed their borders to Jewish refugees who were either fleeing, or had been expelled, from the expanding German Reich.

Sidney Strube, *Daily Express*
17 October 1938

The March of Time

'What! Still having trouble in Palestine?' (The statue of Richard I, Coeur de Lion, speaks to Secretary of State for the Colonies Malcolm MacDonald in front of the Houses of Parliament)

The British United Press reported a 'grave' situation in Palestine, stating that more than 130 Arabs had been killed during the past twenty-four hours in battles with British troops in north Palestine. That brought the number of Arab rebels killed in the past two weeks to nearly 500.

Bernard Partridge, *Punch*
19 October 1938

Allah's Garden

This cartoon reflects the intractability of Malcolm MacDonald's task in finding a solution in Palestine that would suit both the Arabs and the Jews. Derso and Kelen were both Hungarian Jews who were resident artists at the League of Nations during the 1930s.

Alois Derso and Emery Kelen, *Ken Magazine* (United States)
20 October 1938

The Open Door

The accompanying *Time and Tide* diary piece written by East Wind asks: 'What do the Nazis intend with their unfortunate Jewish citizens?' Jews were now excluded from professions and business, and a new ban had been instigated against 'semi-professions, including commercial travellers and salesmen'. The 'Immigration' door is partly opened, albeit inwards, with barbed wire blocking the exit. 'Suicide' is the only way for the non-Aryan.

Victor Weisz 'Vicky', *Time and Tide*
22 October 1938

NOVEMBER FIFTH IN PALESTINE.

Malcolm MacDonald said the government's first duty was 'to establish law and order' and declared that the General Officer Commanding Palestine now had at his disposal 'such forces as were required for the purpose of restoring order, suppressing Arab bandits and re-establishing civil administration in the outlying districts'.

David Low, *Evening Standard*
5 November 1938

No Place to Lay Our Heads

According to the cartoonist: 'Nazi ruthlessness was not confined to air power. Their talents were not restricted to new inventions. For the German Jews a long bitter night began as they became the "whipping boys" for the failures of the German "supermen" and their superior Kultur.'

Daniel Fitzpatrick, *St. Louis Post-Dispatch* (United States)
11 November 1938

It's All a Matter of Finding the Right Tune

In a radio broadcast, Malcolm Macdonald, speaking on the situation in Palestine, said it could only be a matter of time before the activities of the armed rebels and terrorists on both sides were suppressed and law and order re-established. Force by itself, he said, could achieve no solution. The problem of Palestine was to be solved not by military action, but by political action, so that understanding might be reached between the Arabs, Jews and the government. It would be much better to settle this matter by discussion and negotiation.

Cecil Orr, *Daily Record*
14 November 1938

Persecution Plus

On 9 November, the Nazis unleashed a series of pogroms against the Jewish population in Germany and recently incorporated territories. This event came to be called Kristallnacht (The Night of Broken Glass) because of the shattered glass that littered the streets after the vandalism and destruction of Jewish-owned businesses, synagogues and homes.

Ian Gall, *Brisbane Courier-Mail* (Australia)
14 November 1938

The Sporting Touch

By the beginning of 1939, approximately 282,000 Jews had left Germany and 117,000 had left annexed Austria. Of these, some 95,000 emigrated to the United States, 60,000 to Palestine, 40,000 to Great Britain, and about 75,000 to Central and South America, with the largest numbers entering Argentina, Brazil, Chile and Bolivia. More than 18,000 Jews from the German Reich were also able to find refuge in Shanghai, in Japanese-occupied China.

Will Mahony, *Sydney Daily News* (Australia)
14 November 1938

Brown Shirt unit leader reporting to Hitler: 'The lads are very happy, my Führer! They just wonder if we have any other dispensable diplomats abroad.'

The label on the trunk reads: 'Contribution from the Jewish population of Germany'. Depicted on the left is Hermann Goering, who amassed a personal fortune from the confiscation of Jewish property. The shooting dead on 7 November of Ernst vom Rath, a diplomat at the German Embassy in Paris, by Herschel Grynszpan, a seventeen-year-old Polish Jew, served as the excuse for Kristallnacht.

Boris Efimov, *Izvestia* (Soviet Union)
15 November 1938

Where Next?

According to A.G. Gardiner in *John Bull*: 'The civilised world is aflame with horror at the latest phase of Hitler's Jew-baiting mania. The pogrom is the culmination of a policy of racial hate without parallel in magnitude and savagery in human annals ... The immediate question for the civilised world is the problem of helping the victims of the barbarians. One of the greatest obstacles in providing for the fugitives is that they are not only turned adrift, but that they are turned adrift penniless. Gangsterism of the most brazen kind has become the national policy of Germany. The consequence is that their chance of being permitted to take refuge in countries which would give them shelter if they had resources is seriously handicapped.'

George Whitelaw, *Daily Herald*
16 November 1938

Making His Mark!

During Kristallnacht, an estimated 91 Jews were killed, 30,000 Jews arrested and 267 synagogues destroyed.

Harold Talburt, *Washington Daily News* (United States)
16 November 1938

Rousing the Neighbors

In Britain, France and the United States, there was a huge public outcry in response to Kristallnacht. On 15 November, President Roosevelt announced that he had withdrawn the United States' ambassador to Germany. 'I myself could scarcely believe that such things could occur in a twentieth-century civilisation.'

George Finey, *Daily Telegraph* (Australia)
16 November 1938

Sidney Strube, *Daily Express*
16 November 1938

Spitting The Pips Out or Portrait of Mahony's Subconscious

According to the *Belfast Telegraph*: 'Many of the persecuted German Jews have been refused renewal of their passports, and thus have no power or means to leave Germany. Nor is it felt in London that the latest German orders for the most severe penalties against looters of Jewish property presage any abatement in the systematic Nazi drive against the Jews. Rather, it is seen as a determination to preserve these properties intact, probably for confiscation by the State in aid of the national finances.'

Will Mahony, *Sydney Daily News* (Australia)
16 November 1938

Grover Page, *Louisville Courier-Journal* (United States)
20 November 1938

The Long Night

According to Reuters: 'Tunnels, some of them as much as 150 feet long, have been dug under the Franco-German frontier by Jews trying to escape from Germany. Many hundreds of Jews have tried to enter France since the assassination of Herr Vom Rath, but the French frontier guards have been so reinforced that would-be emigrants have to resort to all kinds of subterfuges in order to enter France. Five hundred refugees have been turned back on the French-Saar frontier while about 150 have been allowed to enter. The number who have succeeded in crossing by means of the tunnels, which are dug at night, is unknown. Communes in the Saar which have disposed of all their previous Jewish inhabitants are now flying white flags to show they are "purified".'

Cecil Orr, *Daily Record*
17 November 1938

Wanted: A Christian Answer

Kristallnacht and the increasing brutality of the Nazis' persecution of the Jews horrified many American Christians. On 16 November, Reverend Joseph Corrigan, of the Catholic University of America, said on national radio: 'Where, in the light of the fury of inhumanity raging in Germany … is the tolerance of our vaunted advance in civilisation? Where is the Christianity that once reigned in a Christian nation?' Reverend Peter Ireton then added: 'The world is shocked. Our sense of justice is outraged by the persecution of the Jew in Germany.'

J. Parker Robinson, *Christian Science Monitor*
(United States)
21 November 1938

Guilty on Both Counts

'You are charged (vun) mit being a Jew, und (two) mit letting der mob wreck your premises. Der verdict is guilty trice, und I fine you vun t'ousand million marks. Heil Hitler!'

Norman Lindsay, *Sydney Bulletin* (Australia)
23 November 1938

After the murders and arrests of Kristallnacht, the Nazis accused the Jewish population of having provoked the pogrom and ordered them to pay a billion Reichsmark as punishment. The German tax authorities were ordered to refuse to issue Jews with certificates stating that all their taxes had been paid until the fine had been discharged in full. This meant that no Jew could legally leave Germany, as such a certificate was essential. The original of this cartoon was purchased from the cartoonist by Victor Rothschild.

David Low, *Evening Standard*
23 November 1938

'Answer!'

This cartoon is somewhat ironic considering the Australian government pursued a policy of restricted entry towards Jewish refugees during this period. This was never more evident than at the Evian Conference, where the Australian representative Lieutenant Colonel T.W. White declared that while the fate of Europe's Jews was of 'urgent importance', Australia 'cannot do more' to assist. He declared Australia's position thus: 'It will no doubt be appreciated also that, as we have no real racial problems, we are not desirous of importing one ...'

Aubrey Aria, *The Sun* (Australia)
26 November 1938

In a speech in Berlin the previous May, Hitler had given his thoughts on the Munich peace agreement: 'By 10 October we shall have occupied all German territories which belong to us. Thus, one of the gravest crises has been ended. For the first time we shall be able to look forward to Christmas which shall be a true festival of peace. We all must realise how much we owe to our unity. It amazes me to solve this problem without fighting. How many sacrifices would fighting have demanded? This unity is the strongest guarantor of peace. As long as German people preserve this unity, no one in the world will dare to attack us.'

Kimon Marengo 'Kem', *John Bull*
26 November 1938

Oppression and Suppression

Nazi Bully: 'My will is the will of Germany.'

Bernard Partridge, *Punch*
30 November 1938

Jews Nowhere Welcome Anywhere Anymore

Ahasver: 'By Jehova, by now it seems everybody knows what is wrong, what is the matter with me.'

Rupprecht invented the antisemitic stereotype character 'Ahasver' specifically for *Der Stürmer*. He depicts Ahasver here stating that no one wants the Jews.

Philipp Rupprecht 'Fips', *Der Stürmer* (Germany)
20 December 1938

"How grateful everyone should be to us, that we free such wonderful cultured people and release them to the rest of the world."

Kmoch portrays the Jews as rats who have been expelled from Germany. The democratic states, while expressing sympathy, are seen keeping their gates shut as well. Shortly afterwards, this depiction of Jews as vermin to be exterminated was used in the propaganda film *The Eternal Jew*, to justify the mass murder of Jews in occupied Poland.

Ladislaus Kmoch, *Das Kleine Blatt* (Austria)
2 February 1939

The Palestine Conferences Open in London To-Day

A conference took place at St James's Palace, conducted by Malcolm MacDonald and R.A. Butler, Under-Secretary for Foreign Affairs, to negotiate an agreement between Arabs and Jews in Palestine. The Arab delegates refused to meet directly with the Jewish representatives, which would, to them, have constituted recognition of Jewish claims over Palestine. The British government, therefore, held separate meetings with the two sides. The conference ended in failure on 17 March.

Cecil Orr, *Daily Record*
7 February 1939

'Expound unto me, infidel. How wouldst thou solve the Palestine problem?'

Old Bill, seen here clutching an umbrella, was a popular cartoon character who perhaps personified the practical philosophy of the British soldier on the Western Front during the First World War. He was created by Bruce Bairnsfather and gained widespread fame through his regular appearances in *The Bystander* magazine.

Bruce Bairnsfather, *The Bystander*
1 March 1939

Palestine Conference

'A Difficult Balancing Act'

Britain balancing Arab and Jewish claims in Palestine, with the 'interfering' United States cracking the whip. This cartoon comes from the weekly newspaper of the SS, so its mendacity and its use of antisemitic tropes are no surprise. It portrays the Palestinian Jew as a gangster while the Palestinian Arab is seen as a noble figure. The British are nothing but a tool of American Jewish finance.

Walter Hofmann, *Das Schwarze Korps* (Germany)
3 March 1939

MALCOLM DOES A CHAMBERLAIN

With war in Europe looming, the British government deemed it necessary to appease Palestinian Arabs in order to keep the peace. Malcolm MacDonald therefore prepared a government White Paper which rejected partition and proposed an independent government in Palestine within ten years. With regard to Jewish immigration, no more than 75,000 Jews would be allowed into Palestine in the next five years, after which Jewish immigration would be subject to Arab acquiescence.

David Low, *Evening Standard*
8 March 1939

Hope

The British Refugee Commission proposed British Guiana as a potential Jewish homeland. According to the *Dominica Tribune:* 'In a way the Jew has suffered like the Negro. The Jew has his advantage of being white, and as such he has been able to win greater influence and assistance than the Negro. Why place these two people together to make them become real enemies? The practice of the Jew in British Guiana will naturally bring the enmity of the Negro in that country. Therefore, it would be good for Mr Chamberlain to think seriously over the matter before he allows thousands of Jews to go to British Guiana and to settle there.'

Bob Rodger, *Daily Record*
16 May 1939

Those Terrible Children

The government's White Paper pacified neither Arab nor Jewish opinion in Palestine. The Arabs did not feel the White Paper met their demands for an end to Jewish immigration and so they rejected it. Jews also rejected the White Paper, which they believed would increase hostility between Jews and Arabs and put the Jewish minority at the all-time mercy of the Arab majority. As a result, Zionist groups led a campaign of attacks on government property that lasted several months. On 18 May, a Jewish general strike was called.

Bob Rodger, *Daily Record*
20 May 1939

The Wandering Jew

The S.S. *St. Louis*, a German transatlantic cruise liner, was forced to sail back to Europe after more than 900 of its German Jewish passengers fleeing Nazi persecution were refused entry first to Cuba, then to the United States and Canada. Throughout May and June, newspapers across the United States covered the plight of the refugees on board. However, reactions and opinions varied on the question of the refugees and on the topic of Jewish immigration from Europe.

Edmund Duffy, *Baltimore Sun* (United States)
4 June 1939

Ashamed!

According to the *New York Daily Mirror*, 'The German ship *St. Louis*, with its 907 Jewish refugees, refused entry to Cuba, started slowly back to Germany. They had one brief glimpse of the shores of America, this nation that was built to greatness by immigrants and refugees, this nation whose hospitable hostess has always been that great Statue of Liberty, upon whose base is engraved this welcome:

> Not like the brazen giant of Greek fame,
> With conquering limbs astride from land to land;
> Here at our sea-washed, sunset gates shall stand
> A mighty woman with a torch, whose flame
> Is the imprisoned lightning, and her name
> Mother of Exiles. From her beacon-hand
> Glows world-wide welcome; her mild eyes command
> The air-bridged harbor that twin cities frame.
> 'Keep, ancient lands, your storied pomp,' cries she
> With silent lips. 'Give me your tired, your poor,
> Your huddled masses yearning to breathe free,
> The wretched refuse of your teeming shore.
> Send those, the homeless tempest-tost to me.
> I lift my lamp beside the golden door.'

Our Goddess of Liberty hides her face in shame today as our now stern shores send back this refugee ship.'

Fred L. Packer, *New York Daily Mirror* (United States)
6 June 1939

Rock of Ages, Cleft for Me

'Rock of Ages' is a Christian hymn written by Augustus M. Toplady. Legend has it that the inspiration for this hymn was his own experience of seeking refuge on a rock during a storm.

Jesse Cargill, *King Features Syndicate*
(United States)
7 June 1939

Old Man of the Sea

Illegal Jewish immigration into Palestine was denounced by Mr Malcolm MacDonald in the House of Commons last night during the debate on Palestine policy.

Malcom MacDonald accused the Jewish Agency in Palestine of 'condoning' illegal immigration of Jewish refugees to Palestine. According to the *Daily Herald*, 'It was perfectly clear that the illegal immigration was being organised to wreck the immigration system of Palestine for the sake of wrecking it. The organisers were out to smash the White Paper policy for the sake of smashing it. MacDonald argued that the people who could have the greatest control over the illegal immigration were the Jewish leaders and the Jewish people themselves. If they were so minded, he said, they could reduce it very greatly indeed.'

Talbot Wilfred Ellison, *Birmingham Evening Mail*
21 July 1939

Love's Labour Lost?

The Mandates Committee reject the British proposals for Palestine as not being in conformity with the mandate.

By four votes to three Britain's latest policy for Palestine was rejected by the Permanent Mandates Commission of the League of Nations. The Commission's majority of four stated that they did not feel the policy of the White Paper complied with the original terms of the mandate. The White Paper was to be discussed before the full Council of the League of Nations on 8 September. The outbreak of the Second World War on 3 September, however, suspended any further deliberations.

George Middleton, *Birmingham Gazette*
19 August 1939

He Asked For It!

Germany is begging the Jews to return.

In an article entitled 'Germany begging for Jews to return', the *Sheffield Daily Telegraph* stated that: 'Germany is already promising restitution to Jewish and other refugees of high technical skill if they will return and serve the Fatherland. Posters displayed at the German Consulate in Antwerp urge all doctors, engineers, and other technical experts of German nationality, no matter what their race, to return home and work for Germany again. It is promised that fortunes confiscated from such refugees will be restored if they return... So far, no Jewish technical experts or professional men are known to have responded to the invitation.' This obviously erroneous story appeared in several British newspapers at the time.

Harry Heap, *The Star* (Sheffield)
15 September 1939

The Don't Look Man

The British government published a White Paper revealing sadistic cruelty in Nazi prison camps. It described the appalling treatment, more often than not accompanied by tortures reminiscent of the Spanish Inquisition, meted out to the inmates of concentration camps. It told of 'tree-binding' in Buchenwald, Germany's new 'City of Sorrow', of the 'sweat box', of floggings and hangings. It told of prisoners driven mad by the barbarity and the almost incredible indignities to which they had been submitted.

Wyndham Robinson, *The Star*
1 November 1939

Mein Camp!

'If Halifax declared that he stands for Kultur, then I reply: "In these last six years more has been done for Kultur in Germany than in the last 100 years in Britain."' Hitler

Hitler violently attacked British war aims, screaming: 'If [Lord] Halifax declared that he stands for Kultur, then I reply: "We have had a Kultur at a time when the British had not the slightest idea of Kultur." In these last six years, more has been done for Kultur in Germany than in the last hundred years in Britain. We have built up an army of which there is no equal in the world. This army, backed by a people of such compact unity, is unparalleled in history, and above this army and this people there is a Government with a fanatical willpower similarly without precedent.'

Harold Hodges, *Western Mail*
10 November 1939

POLAND.—LEBENSRAUM FOR THE CONQUERED

Tens of thousands of Jews from Germany and Austria were deported to Lublin after Poland had been occupied by the Nazis. Joseph Goebbels wrote in his diary about these deportations: 'The ghettos which will be emptied in the cities of the General Government will now be refilled with Jews thrown out of the Reich.' According to the *Daily Herald*: 'A fair proportion of the Jews in the reservation come from Western Poland or West Prussia. They were turned out of their homes at a moment's notice and allowed to take nothing but a suitcase which was confiscated on the journey. And the Jews of other centres of Eastern Germany, such as Frankfurt and Oder, have been warned that they will shortly be drafted to Lublin.'

David Low, *Picture Post*
20 January 1940

The Way of an Eagle – German Style

According to the *Daily Telegraph*, a long and detailed report compiled for the Vatican on German atrocities in Poland was published. 'The Germans have resorted to systematic massacres and executions in their attempts to exterminate the population … Particulars are given of public executions which are hardly ever preceded by trials. As a rule the victims are taken from prison and shot outright, and they are never allowed to say good-bye to their families or to receive the comforts of religion. In some cases Roman Catholic victims have been purposely buried in Jewish cemeteries. In other cases, as in one instance at Gdynia, as many as 350 hostages were executed after having been made to dig their graves... The loss of life in the concentration camps is almost as heavy as that from executions and massacres.'

Clive Uptton, *Daily Sketch*
7 February 1940

Dr Frank, Governer- General of the German-occupied part of Poland, declared in a speech in Berlin: 'There is not a concentration camp in the whole of Poland'

Hans Frank was appointed Governor General of Poland, and under his administration the infamous death camps were used to exterminate Jews. As a result he quickly became known as 'The Butcher of Poland'. According to the *Daily Telegraph* and *Morning Post* Amsterdam correspondent: 'To counteract the depression created in neutral countries by reports of the Nazi terror in Poland, Dr Frank, the German Governor General, was summoned to Berlin from Cracow to explain to foreign correspondents that Poland has never been so happy and prosperous. To judge by the reaction in Holland, however, his mission has not been very successful. Dr Frank, a man of notoriously bad character, clearly shows that he regards himself as the representative of a superior people ruling over a conquered colony.'

Sidney Moon, *Sunday Dispatch*
11 February 1940

President Roosevelt sent his closest foreign policy adviser, Sumner Welles, on a tour of four European capitals in order to assess the war situation in Europe. Hitler received Welles and insisted that the Allied war aim was 'annihilation', that of Germany 'peace'. He lectured Welles on all he had done to maintain peace with England and France. According to the Press Association: 'Germany is exploiting the visit of Mr Sumner Welles to Europe to launch a "peace offensive" … Hitler, it is stated, will say that he is ready for peace, but M. Daladier and Mr Chamberlain will declare that they do not want peace. It will then be clear, according to the radio statements, who will bear the responsibility for the continuation of the war.'

Kimon Marengo 'Kem', *John Bull*
24 February 1940

The House of Commons has a full-dress debate on Palestine to-day

Malcolm MacDonald defended the government's implementation of the White Paper on Palestine. This was mainly on the new policy of restricting the sale of Arab lands to Jews. The Labour Party, believing the policy to be contrary to the wishes of the mandate, set down a vote of censure on the government's Palestine land transfer policy, but this was defeated by 292 votes to 129.

Cecil Orr, *Daily Record*
6 March 1940

On 1 April 1941, pro-German Iraqi officers, headed by Rashid Ali al-Kilani, carried out a coup d'état in Iraq, overthrowing the pro-British regime. Iraq soon became a refuge for the Grand Mufti of Jerusalem, who had fled Palestine after the failure of the Arab revolt. Berlin radio claimed that the mufti, now in Baghdad, had issued an appeal to Arabs in Palestine to join in the struggle against the British.

Leslie Illingworth, *Daily Mail*
7 May 1941

Uneasy Seat

Vichy France, despite its official 'armed neutrality', had allowed Germany to use its bases in Syria to send in weapons and supplies to the Iraqis during the previous month's coup d'état. The British hoped such actions would encourage the Turks to enter the war on the Allied side. However, Turkey remained neutral for the rest of the war.

Reg Manning, *Arizona Republic*
(United States)
3 June 1941

Spreading the Lovely Goebbels Stuff

In a speech on 11 September, America's most famous aviator, Charles A. Lindbergh, claimed that the Jews were 'leading America towards war'. Politicians across the political spectrum denounced his speech. Wendell Willkie, the GOP presidential candidate, called it 'the most un-American talk made in my time by any person of national reputation'. President Roosevelt remained silent, but the White House press secretary noted a 'striking similarity' between what Lindbergh said and 'the outpourings of Berlin in the last few days'.

Theodore Geisel 'Dr Seuss', *PM*
(United States)
18 September 1941

Going Down with Colors Flying

The owner of the *Chicago Tribune*, Robert McCormick, was a passionate isolationist who strongly opposed entering the Second World War so as 'to rescue the British Empire'. According to the New York correspondent of the *Daily Mirror*: 'In Chicago citizens are bored by the Isolationist delirium of Colonel Robert McCormick's newspaper, and are defiantly starting a newspaper of their own in which intervention will be preached. Still another sign of Isolationism's precarious health is that its newspapers and spokesmen are now almost crazy with desperation and are making the wildest statements. New York's leading Isolationist newspaper hysterically warns its readers that if Roosevelt remains in power there may be a revolution.'

Rollin Kirby, *New York Post* (United States)
29 September 1941

Postscript to Exodus

'Large numbers of refugees from Germany and other European countries have left Sydney for towns such as Bowral, Katoomba, Mittagong and Bathurst. They are paying high rents and houses have been sold at boom prices in these centres.'

There was strong opposition among Australians towards Jewish refugee migration. Most preferred migration from Britain and opposed the admission of large numbers of refugees for fear they would undermine Australian living standards. This xenophobia was reflected in the White Australia Policy. Many Australians believed that European Jews were different in ethics and morality from the anglicised Jews whom they respected and admired. There was also a fear of economic competition from the refugees at a time of economic hardship. These factors created a sense of hostility to refugees and led to mounting accusations of various malpractices and 'unsavoury behaviour'.

John Frith, *Sydney Bulletin* (Australia)
24 December 1941

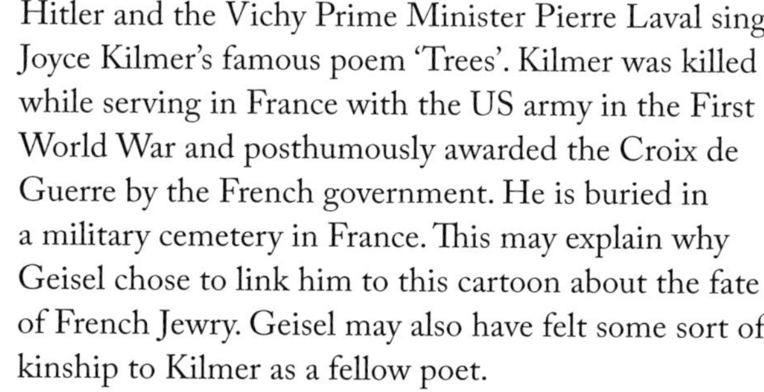

Hitler and the Vichy Prime Minister Pierre Laval sing Joyce Kilmer's famous poem 'Trees'. Kilmer was killed while serving in France with the US army in the First World War and posthumously awarded the Croix de Guerre by the French government. He is buried in a military cemetery in France. This may explain why Geisel chose to link him to this cartoon about the fate of French Jewry. Geisel may also have felt some sort of kinship to Kilmer as a fellow poet.

Theodore Geisel 'Dr Seuss', *PM* (United States)
20 July 1942

Wailing Wall – 1942

It was reported that 300 Jews a day were dying in the Warsaw ghetto. At its height, as many as 460,000 Jews were imprisoned there, in an area of 1.3 square miles, subsisting on meagre food rations. In the summer of 1942, at least 254,000 of the ghetto residents were sent to the Treblinka extermination camp under the guise of 'resettlement in the East'.

Victor Weisz 'Vicky', *News Chronicle*
7 August 1942

"I'VE SETTLED THE FATE OF JEWS" —— "AND OF GERMANS"

A week after this cartoon appeared, Foreign Secretary Anthony Eden told a shocked House of Commons that, according to Polish sources, mass executions of Jews were taking place in occupied Europe, that Jewish ghettos were being 'systematically emptied' and that the able-bodied were being sent to labour camps. After his announcement the House rose and held a one-minute silence in sympathy for the victims. According to the cartoonist: 'Details of the Nazi methods of mass extermination of Jews in Poland by shooting, poison gas and electrocution revealed appalling depths of cold brutality.'

David Low, *Evening Standard*
14 December 1942

Antisemitism was a prevalent attitude in the United States during the war and even more widespread as news of the Holocaust reached America. Antisemitism in the State Department also played a large role in Washington's hesitant response to the plight of European Jews persecuted by the Nazis.

Theodore Geisel 'Dr Seuss', *PM* (United States)
16 December 1942

Warned

In the Commons, Anthony Eden stated that: 'The British and French governments condemn in the strongest possible terms this bestial policy of cold-blooded extermination. They declare that such events can only strengthen the resolve of all freedom loving peoples to overthrow the barbarous Hitlerite tyranny ... They reaffirm their solemn resolution to ensure that those responsible for these crimes shall not escape retribution. [cheers] So far as the responsibility is concerned, I would certainly say it is the intention that all persons who can properly be held responsible for these crimes, whether they are the ringleaders or the actual perpetrators of the outrages, shall be treated alike and brought to book.'

William Furnival, *Lancashire Evening Post*
18 December 1942

The Final Pincer Movement

Not only the high perpetrators of the crimes against the Jews, but also the underlings who cheerfully carry out their orders will be punished.

George Middleton, *Birmingham Gazette*
19 December 1942

Application for Membership

Vichy radio reported that Pierre Laval had said that 'without any equivocation or ambiguity' he wanted a Germany victory: 'I want it so that my country should have a chance of striking the menace and scourge of Bolshevism.' He also announced that the anti-Jewish laws passed in France would be followed by further anti-Jewish measures.

George Butterworth, *Daily Dispatch*
21 December 1942

'I would be sorry if no more Jews were to remain in Germany, for then our younger generation would have no opportunity to learn through personal experience the Jewish danger for the German nation.'

Hitler, 26 March 1936.

Victor Weisz 'Vicky', *News Chronicle*
22 December 1942

On 16 January, the British dispatched heavy bombers to attack Berlin for the first time in fourteen months. On 30 September 1942, Hitler had delivered a speech at the Sportpalast, where he had stated that the extermination of the Jews was revenge for Allied bombing.

Stan Fraydas, *PM* (United States)
20 January 1943

'You can't come in, but when you're dead, we'll punish your murderers!'

Bell Locker, political adviser to the Jewish Agency in Palestine, urged immediate action in an attempt to save the lives of European Jews. 'Palestine,' he contended, 'could take large numbers of refugees immediately.' There was a great shortage of labour for the war effort in Palestine. There were 30,000 Palestinians in the fighting forces, 40,000 in industry, and about 40,000 in agriculture. But new people were needed for the rapidly expanding war effort: 'We feel that it would be inhuman if, because of any political reasons whatsoever, the doors of the Holy Land were closed to the persecuted Jews of the Continent.'

Victor Weisz 'Vicky', *News Chronicle*
29 January 1943

WAILING WALL 1943

On 2 February, the surrender of Field Marshal Paulus to the Russians at Stalingrad proved to be the turning point of the war. After that, the Germans were driven all the way back to Berlin. At the same time, Allied bombing targeting German cities brought further misery and suffering to the German people. As Sir Arthur Harris, head of Bomber Command, said at the start of the bombing campaign against Germany: 'They sowed the wind, and now they are going to reap the whirlwind.'

David Low, *Evening Standard*
8 February 1943

The Archbishop of Canterbury urged the British government to declare its readiness to cooperate in finding an immediate refuge in the British Empire and elsewhere for all Jewish refugees that had fled from Nazi-occupied Europe.

David Low, *Evening Standard*
15 February 1943

'We are not opposed to the creation of a Jewish State ... But the solution may be carried out by humanitarian methods.'

Goebbels

Victor Weisz 'Vicky', *News Chronicle*
18 March 1943

President Roosevelt organised a conference in Bermuda to discuss how to aid Jewish refugees liberated by Allied forces as well as what to do about those who still remained in Nazi-occupied Europe. However, there appeared to be little interest in finding a solution. The conference refused to admit representatives from any of the private Jewish organisations. One British delegate even opposed negotiations with the German government to save the Jews on the grounds that 'many of the potential refugees are empty mouths for which Hitler has no use. [...] It would be relieving Hitler of an obligation to take care of these useless people.' Nothing therefore was achieved as United States immigration quotas were not raised, and the British prohibition on Jewish refugees seeking refuge in Palestine remained intact.

Yosef Bass, *Ha'aretz* (Palestine)
8 April 1943

The Nazis moved to liquidate the Warsaw ghetto. In a desperate last stand, the remaining Jewish inhabitants began a hopeless month-long battle against the Nazis. It was the first time that resistance fighters in an area under German control had staged an uprising. Although the Nazis did destroy the ghetto, the resistance fighters achieved at least one of their goals. The 24-year-old commander of the Jewish resistance fighters, Mordecai Anielewicz, articulated what this was in a letter to a friend shortly before his death. 'My life's dream has been realised,' he said. 'I have lived to see Jewish defence in the ghetto rally its greatness and glory.'

Jacob Burck, *Chicago Daily Times*
(United States)
20 May 1943

Despite continuing reports of mass killings of Jews in Poland and Russia, antisemitism in England remained rife. For example, in London, when a crowd, frightened by a nearby bomb burst, fled into an Underground station, with the result that more than a hundred people were crushed to death, a rumour spread across London that 'the Jews were responsible'. As it was also seen that the Jews would benefit from an Allied victory, a theory developed among many people that they were fighting a 'Jewish war' or, as Hitler had often stated, the Jews had been responsible for starting it.

David Low, *Evening Standard*
18 June 1943

'We're running short of Jews ...'

The cartoonist inscribed this cartoon: 'To the memory of my darling mother – murdered by the Germans somewhere in the Ghettos of Poland.'

Arthur Szyk, *PM* (United States)
20 July 1943

'Refer to Committee 3, Investigation Subcommittee 6, Section 8B, for consideration.'

A news article in *PM* on 29 September had begun: 'One hundred thousand Jews are being killed each month in Poland by the German Government.' The article also quoted a statement issued by Jewish leaders in Warsaw shortly before their deaths, in which they criticised the Allies for not acting to rescue European Jewry: 'Our Allies must realize at last the full extent of the historic responsibility that will fall upon those who have remained inactive in the face of the Nazis' unparalleled crime against an entire people, the tragic epilogue of which is taking place today.'

Eric Gödel, *PM* (United States)
3 October 1943

Evidence for the Prosecution

'No particular geographical location.'

George Middleton, *Birmingham Gazette*
3 November 1943

Letter from Exile

According to a news report reaching Palestine, only one Jew had survived in the city of Kiev when the Soviets liberated it from the Germans in November 1943.

Yosef Bass, *Ha'aretz* (Palestine)
12 November 1943

Time and Blood Are Running Out

The British White Paper policy of May 1939 had prevented all but a trickle of Jewish immigration to Palestine during the war.

Stan MacGovern, *New York Post* (United States)
10 April 1944

'German inventive genius is about to restore the technical equilibrium' – Hitler, 5 July 1944

According to the *Birmingham Daily Post*: 'Details of the fate of more than 400,000 Hungarian Jews who were sent to Poland have been received by the Polish Ministry of the Interior. On 15 May, the Germans deported from Hungary sixty-two railway carriages loaded with Jewish children aged between two and eight years. Since then six trains loaded with Jewish adults have daily passed through the station of Plaszow, near Krakow, bound for Oswiecim, where most of them have been put to death in the gas chambers.'

Victor Weisz 'Vicky', *News Chronicle*
10 July 1944

The Promise Has Been Fulfilled

'Hey, Jews, we've rescued you!'

This cartoon takes direct aim at the claim by Allied leaders that the rescue of concentration camp inmates was secondary to defeating the Germans. Jewish organisations had argued that if rescue was postponed, there would be no Jews left alive by the end of the war, as the Allied soldier in the cartoon discovers when he arrives to save the Jews. The gravestone reads 'Here lies European Jewry'.

Yehoshua Adan, *Haboker* (Palestine)
19 July 1944

What Will We Do About the Other 480,000?

In the summer of 1944, the Hungarian police force, under the guidance of German SS officials, deported approximately 440,000 Jews from Hungary to Auschwitz-Birkenau, where, upon arrival and after selection, SS functionaries killed the majority of them in gas chambers. Unlike in this cartoon, 20,000 visas were not forthcoming and the borders of Palestine remained closed to refugees.

A.W. MacKenzie, *New York Post* (United States)
19 August 1944

The Weight of Evidence

A United States opinion poll showed that the average American had come to believe what they had been told about German atrocities. To the question 'Do you believe the stories that the Germans have murdered many people in concentration camps are true or not true?', 76 per cent thought the stories were true. Only 12 per cent thought they were not, while 12 per cent did not know. When the 76 per cent were asked to estimate how many people the Germans had murdered, they came up with some strange responses. The largest group (27 per cent) thought it was 100,000 or fewer. Four per cent said 6,000,000 or more.

Roy Justus, *Minneapolis Star* (United States)
1 December 1944

The Crime No Punishment Can Fit

The *News Chronicle* stated that overwhelming evidence had been accumulated of 'murder and bestial' tortures committed by Germans in occupied Europe: 'No retribution can be too harsh or harsh enough for the creatures who have perpetrated these infamies.'

Anne Mergen, *Dayton News* (United States)
2 December 1944

Coming Events

Two Jewish Palestinian youths, Eliyahu Bet-Zuri and Eliyahu Hakim, were hanged for the murder in Cairo of Lord Moyne, British Minister Resident in the Middle East. The killing was condemned by Jewish leaders and newspapers in Britain and Palestine, but significant damage was done to the Zionist cause. Winston Churchill was particularly upset that 'Jewish terrorists' had killed his personal friend at a time when he believed he had been fighting a lonely struggle on behalf of the Zionist cause.

J.C. Walker, *News of the World*
20 January 1945

Hitler spent his last days in his bunker in Berlin. It was Heinrich Heine who had said, 'Those who burn books will in the end burn people.' According to Winston Churchill, Hitler and Eva Braun 'were burnt in the courtyard, and Hitler's funeral pyre, with the din of the Russian guns growing ever louder, made a lurid end of the Third Reich'.

Victor Weisz 'Vicky', *News Chronicle*
16 April 1945

'Master Race'

As the Allies continued to liberate the death camps, the full unimaginable horror of the Nazis' 'Final Solution' for European Jewry became all too apparent.

Ian Gall, ***Brisbane Courier-Mail*** (Australia)
20 April 1945

The Hunt Is On

In the Commons, Churchill responded to further evidence of the Nazi genocide of the Jews by saying: 'No words can express the horror which is felt by H.M. Government and their Allies at the proof of these frightful crimes now daily coming into view.' Churchill added that a solemn warning had been prepared that not only the men at the top would be held accountable, but also those people who had carried it out with their own hands. Churchill made it clear that no order from a superior authority would be any form of shield for them.

George Middleton, *Birmingham Gazette*
21 April 1945

'The Fuehrer [sic] was distressed to read of your plight – he sends you part of his birthday presents to give you new hope. Heil Hitler!'

Stephen Roth, *Sunday Pictorial*
22 April 1945

Inside Germany

'Why don't you Americans mind your own business? This is strictly an internal German affair.'

American troops forced German townspeople to witness the inside of many of the death camps and often forced them to carry the bodies of dead prisoners to mass graves for burial.

Eric Gödel, *PM* (United States)
29 April 1945

Witnesses for the Prosecution

According to the cartoonist: 'Judgement day was drawing near for the Nazi operators of gas chambers, bake ovens, and other forms of mass civilian murder. When the swift American armored units caught such places as Buchenwald unawares, unbelievable conditions were uncovered.'

Daniel Fitzpatrick, *St. Louis Dispatch* (United States)
30 April 1945

The Himmler Salute

After hearing that Heinrich Himmler had attempted to transmit an offer of surrender to the commander-in-chief of the Allied forces, Hitler stripped him of all his offices and ordered his immediate arrest.

Victor Weisz 'Vicky', *News Chronicle*
30 April 1945

And the World Will Remember

Joseph Goebbels was quoted in *Das Reich* declaring that the war had passed its climax, and that it would have a sudden end: 'It does not behove man to reason with war or to speculate what course may be. War enters the scene with the elementary fury of nature and leaves it again in most cases quite suddenly after a last paroxysm of fury. Right to the end fighting will remain fluid, with every one of the belligerents trying until the very last hour to force victory to his side.'

George Butterworth, *Daily Dispatch*
2 May 1945

After Hitler committed suicide on 30 April, there was a fear that somehow Nazism would revive itself once the war had ended. Like Vicky, Zec was conscious of being Jewish and consequently would never point directly to the main victims of the Holocaust. This was in case, I assume, readers accused them of prioritising Jewish suffering over the many other victims of the war.

Philip Zec, *Daily Mirror*
3 May 1945

Wartime Portrait of a 'Good German'

According to the *Daily Record*: 'German civilians who have been marched by the US military authorities to the Buchenwald concentration camp to see the conditions there have shown no indication of shame or remorse. Lord Stanhope, leader of the Parliamentary delegation to the camp, told the Lords that the women who visited the camp crematorium expressed the attitude, "It is nothing to do with me and I don't care." Lord Addison, also a member of the delegation, said that although he was convinced the majority of the German people knew what was going on at the camp, he saw no signs whatever of shame among the Germans who visited it. Lord Vansittart said that this time there was no possibility of denying the German atrocities but a new excuse was being put up. It was that they did not know about it, which was profoundly untrue. The German nation had lived on slave labour and revelled in it.'

John Francis Knott, *Dallas Morning News*
(United States)
6 May 1945

For This I Fought Hitler?

The Tory MP for Peebles, Captain Archibald Ramsay, wanted to reintroduce the medieval Statute of Jewry, which was repealed in 1846. The Statute made the wearing of a yellow star compulsory and denied Jews social intercourse with Christians. Ramsay's motion said the Statute 'protected His Majesty's subjects from Jewish extortion and exploitation', and added that 'these evils have become a grievous menace'. An official of the Board of Deputies of British Jews commented: 'This is an attempt to introduce into this country laws similar to those of the Nazis.' Ramsay had been the only MP to be interned under the Defence Regulations 18B. Most of the members of the British Union of Fascists were also held under this law during the war.

George Whitelaw, *Daily Herald*
1 June 1945

The Weed

News emerged of continuing antisemitic outrages across Europe. This was particularly the case in Poland, where anti-Jewish pogroms were carried out against Polish Jews who returned after surviving the death camps.

William Timyn 'Tim', *John Bull*
8 September 1945

Once Upon a Time

On 17 September, the trial opened of Josef Kramer, the commandant of the Belsen concentration camp. He had been in charge there since December 1944, having previously been a senior camp administrator at Auschwitz, where he oversaw many of the gassings of Jews at Birkenau. Towards the end of the war, Belsen had been a reception camp for many of the prisoners removed from camps further east as the Soviet Army advanced, resulting in the chronic overcrowding, starvation and disease discovered by the British liberating forces. These conditions were made even worse by Kramer's brutal regime, which earned him the nickname the 'Beast of Belsen'. Kramer was sentenced to death for crimes both at Auschwitz and at Bergen-Belsen, and was hanged on 13 December 1945.

George Whitelaw, *Daily Herald*
18 September 1945

No Promised Land

For hundreds of thousands of Jewish survivors of the Holocaust, the war did not end in September 1945. The refugees from Eastern Europe and the liberated concentration camps, unwilling or unable to return home, were forced into displaced persons (DP) camps in defeated Germany under Allied protection.

Victor Weisz 'Vicky', *News Chronicle*
20 September 1945

General George Patton was criticised by General Eisenhower for slowness in rooting out Nazis in Bavaria. Patton said that while he believed that there were no Nazis left in important positions in Bavaria, only 50,000 of the 400,000 persons scheduled for removal had so far been sacked. The general explained that if they were all turned out before other people had been trained to take their places, the occupation forces would find themselves responsible for starving and freezing women, old men and children.

Eric Gödel, *PM* (United States)
24 September 1945

HE PREFERS SAND-CASTLES

According to the cartoonist: 'UN special envoy Count Folke Bernadotte wrote about the "amazing work the Jews had done in cultivating this desert-like countryside ... and the very sharp lines of demarcation between the desert on the one hand and the fertile gardens and orange groves on the other". Bernadotte appeared to be unaware that what he had witnessed – the coastal plain from Haifa to Tel Aviv – was the most fertile part of the country, and that more than half of it was owned by the indigenous population. Low was clearly influenced by the romantic idea that Jewish settlers had made the 'desert bloom'. Zionist propagandists had claimed that Palestine had lain destitute before being cultivated by Jewish settlers.

David Low, *Evening Standard*
28 September 1945

'We appear to be treating the Jews as the Nazis treated them, except that we do not exterminate them.'
Harrison report to President Truman

Earl Harrison is best known for the report bearing his name that examined the plight of Holocaust survivors in DP camps in post-war Europe. His report offered scathing criticism of the DPs' treatment. Many were living under armed guard behind barbed wire, sometimes in the very camps where they had been victimised, in crowded and unsanitary accommodation in marked contrast to the living conditions of the German population. The Jewish DPs faced restrictions on their movement, could not obtain information about their relatives, had nothing to occupy their time, and lacked any representative to advocate for them with military authorities.

Eric Gödel, *PM* (United States)
1 October 1945

According to the *Daily Dispatch:* 'Dr Alexander Altmann, Communal Rabbi of Manchester and Salford, whose parents were put to death in the gas chambers of Auschwitz, protested that the government had not appointed Jewish liaison officers to help displaced Jews in liberated areas. "Jews," he said, "are living under shocking conditions. These unfortunate human beings have been liberated, but for them there is no liberation. They have only one hope – that the gates of Palestine will be opened to them."'

Eric Gödel, *PM* (United States)
2 October 1945

Use No Naked Lights!

The Iraqi premier, General Hamdi al Pachachi, protested to the US government against any intervention in the Palestine question contrary to the rights of the Palestine Arabs. Referring to reports of increasing US pressure on the British government to repudiate the Palestine White Paper and of President Truman's request to Britain to open Palestine to Jewish immigration, the Iraqi premier asserted that this was contrary to US promises that the US would make no move in Palestine before consulting the Arabs.

W.H. Woodburn 'Hengest', *Manchester Evening News*
2 October 1945

President Truman repeatedly called for the British government to allow 100,000 Jewish refugees, the approximate number of DPs in Europe at the time, into Palestine. Responding to Truman's pleas to admit more Jews, Clement Attlee proposed a joint commission to resolve the crisis. The Anglo-American Committee of Inquiry was established to review the issue of Jewish immigration to Palestine. The committee heard testimony from witnesses in Washington, London, Europe and the Middle East. Zionists demanded the immediate establishment of a Jewish Commonwealth in Palestine. Arabs, on the other hand, called for the establishment of an independent Arab state and an end to Jewish immigration, as well as a cessation of all land sales to Jews.

Leslie Illingworth, *Daily Mail*
8 October 1945

What a Welcome!

What *Jewish Radio* called 'a new period in active resistance' began when a force of 1,000 armed Jews attacked the Atlit clearance camp near Haifa and set free 200 Jewish refugees. A British official communiqué stated that the attack on Atlit was carried out by 'a large number of Jews armed with rifles, pistols, and daggers', who escaped in the direction of Mount Carmel with 208 freed detainees.

George Whitelaw, *Daily Herald*
2 November 1945

Distemper

The *American Press* Jerusalem correspondent said the outbreak of violence in Tel Aviv followed a mass demonstration in which between 40,000 and 50,000 people participated, shouting, 'Down with the White Paper, Attlee and Bevin!' British troops were called into action in Tel Aviv to quell the rioting. Several hundred Jewish youths in Jerusalem stoned bus drivers as a protest against them working during the general strike.

George White, *Tampa Tribune* (United States)
4 November 1945

Foreign Secretary Ernest Bevin was unsure how to relieve distressed and displaced Jews in Europe and reach an accommodation on Palestine between Arab and Jew. He described the problem as 'the most baffling in the world'. As well as this, he had to deal with other issues in the Near East, such as rioting in Egypt and India and a Soviet incursion into Iran.

Leslie Illingworth, *Daily Mail*
23 November 1945

'Attend Unto My Cry!'

In the Old Testament, Psalm 61 begins with a humble request to God: 'Hear my cry, O God; listen to my prayer.' It is a prayer offered up when a person is going through difficult circumstances and feeling overwhelmed. The United States Senate passed, by an overwhelming vote, a resolution favouring unrestricted Jewish immigration into Palestine as a prospective Jewish national home.

Daniel Fitzpatrick, *St. Louis Dispatch* (United States)
19 December 1945

The Line Forms at the Right

Palestine was not the only part of the British Empire that Britain was struggling to maintain. In Egypt, India, Malay and Africa, independence movements were gaining traction in their repeated demands for decolonisation.

Jerry Doyle, *Philadelphia Inquirer* (United States)
23 February 1946

My Sons, My Sons!

According to the *Daily Herald*: 'The report of the Anglo-American Committee of Inquiry has already been hotly criticised by both Zionists and Arabs. That is not surprising, since the Committee recommends that Palestine shall become neither a Jewish State nor an Arab one. Yet the Committee could have come to no other conclusion without doing violent injustice to either the Jews or the Arabs. And it is to be hoped that both sides will realise that they have, at this hour, a responsibility not only to themselves but to Humanity … The Committee proposes for Palestine self-government in which Arab and Jew will enjoy equal status.'

W.H. Woodburn 'Hengest', *Manchester Evening News*
1 May 1946

Holding the Babies

The Anglo-American Committee of Inquiry declared its opposition to the White Paper of 1939, which had severely limited Jewish immigration to Palestine. The committee supported Truman's original proposal that 100,000 European Jews should be immediately allowed in. Celebrations among Jewish refugees in the internment camps were short-lived. The British Mandate Authority rejected the proposal, stating that such immigration was impossible while armed conflict in Palestine persisted. Despite American, Jewish and international pressure and the recommendations of the Anglo-American Committee of Inquiry, Bevin continued to enforce the policy as outlined in the White Paper.

George Whitelaw, *Daily Herald*
3 May 1946

Clement Attlee came under criticism for requesting help from the United States in implementing the policy of the Anglo-American Report. According to the *Yorkshire Post*: 'Attlee's proposal that the United States should give military and financial aid in Palestine has, of course, its critics. Two American members of the Anglo-American Committee of Inquiry have criticised Attlee for making immigration conditional on the disarming of secret armed forces. They said the Committee had considered and rejected such a condition on the grounds that it was inhuman and impossible of fulfilment.'

Victor Weisz 'Vicky', *News Chronicle*
6 May 1946

And Pharaoh Hardened His Heart

King Farouk of Egypt informed the British government that the Mufti of Jerusalem was in Cairo, and that he had been given sanctuary there. The mufti had put himself at the mercy of the king, and it was an Arab and Muslim tradition that when a man goes to the palace and asks for the king's protection the king must give it. Churchill asked what measures the British government proposed to take to apprehend the mufti, who had been a 'marked enemy of the Allies during the war'. The government stated that ideally it wanted to have the mufti in custody, so as to prevent his return to Palestine.

W.H. Woodburn 'Hengest', *Manchester Evening News*
21 June 1946

Operation Crossroads

Clement Attlee said it had become increasingly clear that acts of Jewish terrorism and sabotage formed part of a concerted plan prepared and executed by a highly developed military organisation with widespread ramifications. Attlee criticised the Jewish Agency, which he felt had too close a working relationship with the Haganah, the Jewish defence organisation, and indirectly with other terrorist bodies. A recurrence of terrorist activity and a campaign of violence had caused the death of sixteen British soldiers and five policemen, including seven soldiers murdered in cold blood in Tel Aviv, and material damage exceeding £4 million. 'We had a mandatory duty to maintain law and order,' Attlee said, 'and could no longer tolerate that challenge to our authority without abdicating our responsibility.'

George Butterworth, *Daily Dispatch*
3 July 1946

Through Which Needle's Eye?

The British government was taken aback by President Truman's unilateral announcement that the US was prepared to assume technical and financial responsibility for transporting 100,000 Jewish refugees from Europe to Palestine. Clement Attlee stated that until Jewish armies in Palestine were disarmed, no large-scale immigration could be allowed. However, US officials indicated that the Truman administration would not be prepared to assist in the disarmament of such illegal armies.

In the New Testament, Jesus is quoted as saying that 'it is easier for a camel to go through the eye of a needle than for a rich man to enter the kingdom of God'. The saying was a response to a rich young man who had asked Jesus what he needed to do to inherit eternal life. Jesus replied, 'If you want to be perfect, go, sell your possessions and give to the poor, and you will have treasure in heaven.'

Victor Weisz 'Vicky', *News Chronicle*
4 July 1946

Till the Sands of the Desert Grow Cold?

The title of the cartoon is from a 1911 song by Ernest Ball and George Graff which has biblical references that profess one's endless love while standing alone in a desert. It emphasises Britain and America's willingness to find a solution without really knowing how to go about doing so.

Ian Gall, *News of the World*
7 July 1946

'I Don't Like Attlee's Policy'

Jewish Congressman Emanuel Celler said that he was introducing an amendment which would withhold the US loan to Britain until the British government had given a definite assurance that 100,000 Jews would be immediately allowed into Palestine. According to the *Dundee Courier*: 'Leading Jews in the US are opposed to endangering the economic interest of the US, Britain and the world just because of a specific grievance which US Jews may have against the British government, even if that grievance were legitimate. Any bid to halt the agreement would be an example of the Jews cutting off their noses to spite their faces.'

Herbert Block 'Herblock', *Washington Post* (United States)
8 July 1946

The King David Hotel was the British administrative and military headquarters in Palestine; it also served as the headquarters of the British Criminal Investigation Division. On 29 June, the British authorities carried out a raid on the Jewish Agency and confiscated a large number of documents. At the same time, approximately 2,500 Jews were arrested. Members of the Jewish underground military group, the Irgun, targeted the hotel both in revenge and as a way of destroying the documents. The leader of the Irgun, Menachem Begin, claimed that he saw the hotel solely as a military building and therefore a legitimate target. The bombing of the hotel on 22 July killed ninety-one people, most of them civilians, and injured forty-five others.

Leslie Illingworth, *Daily Mail*
23 July 1946

The Vandal

The bombing of the King David Hotel, which also killed Jews working at the hotel, provoked outrage throughout the world. However, Menachem Begin claimed that the British authorities had ignored warnings delivered the day before.

George Whitelaw, *Daily Herald*
25 July 1946

Brothers, Brothers, This Is Not the Way to Help Us!

Referring to the King David Hotel bombing, Britain's deputy prime minister, Herbert Morrison, said: 'The curse of Hitler was not yet wholly removed. Some of his victims fleeing from ravaged Europe carried with them germs of those very plagues from which they sought protection. Zionism is regarded by its supporters as an expression of a profound and splendid impulse in the Jewish people's souls. Let them beware lest this modern perversion of their faith bring ruin on them. The leaders of the Jewish community in Palestine, we feel bound to say, have failed to preserve their movement from the contagion of these false ideals. Many of them seem to have been led into courses which their own consciences must have at first condemned.'

(Unpublished) Victor Weisz 'Vicky', *News Chronicle*
25 July 1946

After the King David Hotel bombing, Lieutenant General Sir Evelyn Hugh Barker, British Commander-in-Chief, sent out a circular stating: 'The Jewish community cannot be absolved from responsibility, and I am determined that they should suffer punishment and be made aware of the contempt and loathing with which we regard their conduct. The troops will be punishing the Jews in a way that the race dislikes as much as any – by striking at their pockets.' The Army Council did not punish the general but decided to advise him that his circular was regarded as unfortunate, and that it was not for the military commander to issue political statements. After questions were asked in the House of Commons, Attlee declared that the government had dissociated itself from the actual terms of the letter, and announced that the matter had been placed in the hands of Lord Montgomery.

Victor Weisz 'Vicky', *News Chronicle*
1 August 1946

SEARCH FOR AN OPEN DOOR

According to the cartoonist: 'A million and a half displaced persons still remained in Europe. It was evident that new homes must be found overseas for large numbers, and member governments of the United Nations were asked each to receive a proportion, including Jews. Britain had already accepted and promised to promote resettlement of about 300,000, the US 275,000, and more were to go to South American countries. But plans elsewhere lagged. The question of the limits of Palestine's capacity to receive new immigrants without political and economic upheaval was being argued with guns.'

David Low, *Evening Standard*
2 August 1946

Attlee asked for American support for the Morrison-Grady Plan, which was for the creation of a unitary federal trusteeship in Palestine. This was set up in July 1946 by British and American representatives, headed by Herbert Morrison, then Lord President of the Council, and T. Grady of the US State Department. It claimed to be based on the report of the Anglo-American Committee, and according to Morrison the success of the plan would depend upon American cooperation.

Leslie Illingworth, *Daily Mail*
6 August 1946

"SORRY, THE GIRL-FRIEND'S CHANGED MY MIND"

In the United States, President Truman's initial support for the Morrison-Grady plan changed when American Zionists lobbied against it well before the November mid-term elections. The pressure from American Zionists resulted in Truman rejecting the plan, despite it having been proposed by his own appointee.

David Low, *Evening Standard*
7 August 1946

A Policeman's Lot ...

The cartoon emphasises the difficulties faced by Britain in attempting to pacify both the Jews and the Arabs while, at the same time, not alienating the Americans whose loans to Britain were stopping the country from going bankrupt.

Aubrey Aria, *Daily Sun* (Australia)
11 August 1946

Stop Shoving at the Back There

A group of American Congressmen, members of the League for a Free Palestine, demanded that not only should the partition plan advocated by the British government be dropped, but insisted on the admission to Palestine of 100,000 Jewish refugees as recently requested by President Truman.

W.H. Woodburn 'Hengest', *Manchester Evening News*
13 August 1946

According to the *Daily News*: 'Orders to establish camps on Cyprus to hold 10,000 illegal immigrants have been given by the Governor of Cyprus. Under extraordinary powers, the Governor may detain any person brought into the colony by the Navy, Army or Air Force and certified by the officer in charge of the escort to be an illegal immigrant. Immigrants may be moved, if necessary by force, from a vessel or aircraft. Police may arrest without warrant an illegal immigrant escaping. Escape may be punished by imprisonment for three years and a fine of £100. A Jewish Agency spokesman declared that Jewish immigration was continuing even if it meant immigration to Cyprus.'

Leslie Illingworth, *Daily Mail*
15 August 1946

The Wandering Jew, 1946

According to the cartoonist: 'Shiploads of Jewish migrants from all over Europe were being intercepted off the coast of Palestine and the miserable passengers diverted to concentration camps in Cyprus. Refused entry into Britain, America and Palestine, still the victims of antisemitic attacks, the Jews remain the great tragedy of the world.'

Jimmy Friell 'Gabriel', *Daily Worker*
20 August 1946

According to the *Daily News*: 'When the first batch of 1,300 illegal immigrants, escorted from Haifa by the cruiser *Ajax*, were disembarked at the Cyprus port of Famagusta, they shouted, "Palestine! Palestine! Bevin is like Hitler and Mussolini." More than 1,400 Jewish illegal immigrants lying off Haifa in two ships last night were reported on hunger strike.' According to the *Scotsman*: 'Soldiers helped the weak to board the transport and carried those unable to walk. The majority needed help. When the immigrants saw the Press party, one gave a hysterical speech and several shouted in unison, "Heil Bevin, Heil Hitler."'

William Gropper, *Daily Worker* (United States)
10 September 1946

The Irgun carried out a series of terrorist attacks throughout Palestine in protest against the London conference. This had been convened after the Arabs had dismissed the Anglo-American report. The conference was supposed to consist of Jewish and Arab leaders, in order to resolve the future of Palestine and negotiate an end to the mandate. Only representatives of the Arab states attended, as it was boycotted by both Jewish and Palestinian Arab representatives.

Leslie Illingworth, *Daily Mail*
11 September 1946

It's All Yours, Ernest

W.H. Woodburn 'Hengest',
Manchester Evening News
24 September 1946

According to the *Aberdeen Journal*: 'Members of the British Embassy staff in Washington on going to work yesterday found a Union Jack with a large black swastika painted on it at the Embassy gates. The flag also bore the words: "America 1776, Palestine 1946 – Dachau, Buchenwald, Cyprus".'

William Gropper, *Daily Worker* (United States)
8 October 1946

Divide and Rule

Many on the far left saw America's call for a temporary trusteeship over Palestine instead of partition as both an attempt to deny Palestinian Jews and Arabs their right to self-determination and an opportunity to maintain colonial rule over the country.

Herbert McClintock, *Tribune* (Australia)
15 October 1946

According to the *Daily Mail*, members of the Stern gang had threatened to assassinate Field Marshal Bernard Montgomery unless the British policy in Palestine was changed. The threat to his life was made over the telephone to the War Office. The reason why Montgomery was placed on a death list by the terrorists was that it was known that the field marshal had resisted for some time the call in Parliament to have General Barker removed from his post in Palestine.
(See cartoon: 1 August 1946 regarding General Barker.)

Leslie Illingworth, *Daily Mail*
12 November 1946

U.N.O. TO RUN PALESTINE (latest suggestion)

Senator Claude Pepper (Democrat, Florida) told the Executive Committee of the American Jewish Congress that the United States should demand intervention in Palestine by the United Nations: 'Let us remove Britain's mandatory power over Palestine and put that unfortunate country under the protection of the United Nations. The United Nations should put a force in Palestine to do whatever is needed to keep the peace.'

W.H. Woodburn 'Hengest', *Manchester Evening News*
13 November 1946

Soldiers' Luck

'Rum blokes these! First we fight a war to save them, and then they blow us up.'

Members of the Irgun gang blew up the British Embassy in Rome in retaliation for the deportation of illegal Jewish immigrants from Palestine. The bombing was the first terrorist operation by the Irgun against British personnel in Europe.

Ernest H. Shepard, *Punch*
20 November 1946

"WHAT, HE'S NOT ANTI-SEMITIC? WE'LL SOON ALTER THAT."

Despite the wave of Jewish 'terrorist' action against British soldiers and policemen in Palestine, British Home Secretary James Chuter Ede believed the majority of Jews were against these terrorist attacks. In the Commons he stated: 'I am quite convinced that the overwhelming majority of Jews throughout the world deprecate the action that a very limited number have taken.'

David Low, *Evening Standard*
22 November 1946

'Just one more killing, then I'll come help with the house.'

Bill Mauldin, *St. Louis Dispatch* (United States)
25 November 1946

According to the *Manchester Evening News*: 'It is impossible to find any excuse for the latest action of the Jewish terrorists in Palestine: the flogging of four British soldiers – whatever the pretext – was an outrage that will be condemned throughout the civilised world, and has, indeed, already been condemned by responsible Jewish leaders in Palestine [...]It is necessary to seek out and punish the terrorists who are responsible for this and other crimes, but to suggest that this is all that need be done is an over-simplification of the problem that will get us nowhere.'

W.H. Woodburn 'Hengest', *Manchester Evening News*
30 December 1946

Overdrawn

Following the publication of this cartoon, the 17 January edition of the Australian *Jewish Herald* contained a letter from Rabbi Dr E. Berkovits, Chief Minister of the Central Synagogue, Sydney, to the *Sydney Morning Herald*. Rabbi Berkovits claimed that the cartoon was typical of the 'Sturmer' technique. 'What a pity,' he wrote, 'that poor Streicher was hanged so precipitately. He would have greatly admired your cartoon.' Berkovits then went on to say it was not the Bank of 'World Sympathy' but the Bank of 'World Justice' that the Jews were trying to contact.

John Frith, *Sydney Morning Herald* (Australia)
2 January 1947

THE DARK MIRROR

The escalation in violence in Palestine and the murder of British soldiers by the Irgun and Stern gangs created a wave of revulsion back in Britain. Creech Jones, the Colonial Secretary, told the president of the Jewish Agency in Palestine, David Ben Gurion, that the British government demanded the outlawing of the Irgun and Stern terrorists by Palestinian Jewry. Ben Gurion was warned of the serious damage the actions of the Jewish terrorists were wreaking on British public opinion.

David Low, *Evening Standard*
3 January 1947

On 27 January, a British judge, Ralph Windham, was kidnapped from his courtroom in Tel Aviv in retaliation for the death sentence imposed by the British authorities on Dov Gruner, a member of the Irgun. Windham was eventually released when the authorities gave in to the kidnappers' demands: the release of Gruner and other Jewish detainees.

Leslie Illingworth, *Daily Mail*
29 January 1947

'The Partition of Palestine'

The following letter was sent by a reader to the *Melbourne Argus*, which refused to print it:
'I am writing to express regret at the publication of Mr Armstrong's cartoon, "The Partition of Palestine". The cartoon is a graphic presentation of a half-truth, and is thus all the more perfidious. That terrorist activities are prejudicial to Jewish interests is admitted, but the cartoon conceals the fact that terrorism is deprecated and repudiated by world-wide Jewry, and is strongly discountenanced by religious Jews even in Palestine itself. If Australia nationally had been accused and stigmatised for the alleged actions of a few Australians, how our indignation would justly have been aroused! Why, then, should Israel nationally be stigmatised for the actions of the minority? Again, at a time when the twin harlots, Fascism and antisemitism, beckon for their degenerate customers, I draw attention to the slight upon Jewry conveyed in the offensive figure in the cartoon ... Finally, the cartoon is a gross perversion of the truth, and whilst uniting with world Jewry in deprecating terrorism, we must admit that the prime cause springs from broken pledges made to the Jewish people.'

Mick Armstrong, *Melbourne Argus* (Australia)
31 January 1947

Hold It!

After a frustrating final meeting with the Arab delegation at the London conference, Ernest Bevin announced that the British government would be referring the Palestine problem to the United Nations Organisation. The Foreign Secretary said this decision had been made because no proposal put forward by them had proved acceptable as basis for further discussion. The leader of each Arab delegation re-emphasised that no proposal which involved any form of partition or Jewish immigration would be acceptable. In November 1945, Bevin had said he would stake his political future on solving the Palestine problem.

George Butterworth, *Daily Dispatch*
20 February 1947

Here – You Try It!

On the news that Britain had referred Palestine to the United Nations, the Jewish Agency responded by stating: 'We don't mind. The only thing is that if it goes to the United Nations Organisation they will want to know why the Mandate has not been fulfilled. It will take at least nine or ten months if it goes to the UN and the position in Palestine will deteriorate unless, of course, the provisions of the Mandate are carried out in accordance with international law, and the 1939 White Paper, which is in conflict with the Mandate, is repealed.

Ian Gall, *News of the World*
23 February 1947

A Camel's All Lumpy, and Bumpy and Humpy …

The caption is a quotation from a children's poem entitled 'The Camel's Complaint' by Charles Edward Carryl.

Victor Weisz 'Vicky', *News Chronicle*
25 February 1947

On 4 May, a mass breakout occurred at Acre prison in an operation undertaken by the Irgun. The former citadel contained 700 Arab prisoners and ninety Jewish prisoners, the latter mainly members of the Jewish underground groups Haganah, Lehi and Irgun, who had been captured by the British. Twenty-seven Irgun prisoners escaped along with 214 Arab prisoners after a hole was blown in the main wall of the citadel. It was reported the day after that Jews were saying the breach of Acre prison 'was something that Napoleon could not do when Sir Sydney Smith held Acre fortress against him in 1799'. The storming of Acre prison has been credited as a critical event that led to Britain's decision to end the mandate in Palestine.

Leslie Illingworth, *Daily Mail*
6 May 1947

'Shameful the way the British are handling this Palestine business.'

The British government protested over US press advertisements calling for funding for illegal immigration and underground armies in Palestine as well as promoting violence in that country. It came soon after Lord Inverchapel, British ambassador, delivered an aide memoire to the Foreign Office specifically protesting recent New York press advertisements urging terrorists in Palestine to increase their actions against British troops and installations there. Truman responded by stating: 'I urge all citizens meticulously to refrain, while the United Nations are considering the problem of Palestine, from engaging in or facilitating any activities which tend further to inflame the passions of the inhabitants of Palestine to undermine law and order or to promote violence in that country.'

Carl Giles, *Daily Express*
8 June 1947

TRAFFIC IN MISERY

American Zionists funded many of the sixty ships that attempted to take illegal Jewish refugees, mostly Holocaust survivors, to Palestine. *Exodus 1947* was the largest of them, carrying more Jewish refugees than any other. Although it had been built to carry 400 passengers along with fifty crew, 4,515 passengers were stuffed aboard with hundreds of crew members. The British decision to send this ship back to Europe instead of detaining its passengers in Cyprus represented an admission of the failure of the Cyprus deterrent. For most of those survivors interned in Cyprus, the experience only served to strengthen their resolve to reach Palestine, which they almost all did following the creation of Israel in May 1948.

David Low, *Evening Standard*
31 July 1947

The Wailing Wall

The *News Chronicle* was critical of Britain's administration in Palestine for its two years of 'inaction' and 'witless drifting'. According to the newspaper: 'A year ago it seemed almost impossible that the situation in Palestine could further deteriorate ... On February 18 Mr. Ernest Bevin told the House of Commons that his Majesty's Government could accept neither Jewish nor Arab proposals, had no solution of its own to impose and so had decided to submit the problem to the judgment of the United Nations... The Jewish Agency demanded the immediate provision of sanctuary inside Palestine for the distressed remnants of European Jewry, who, two years after the end of the war, are still rotting away in camps in Germany and Austria. At any time during the past two years a decision to permit even 100,000 of the Jewish survivors to enter Palestine, over a reasonably lengthy period, would have brought an immediate end to Jewish-made disorder. And of one year ago the decision would have caused no Arab disorders.'

Victor Weisz 'Vicky', *News Chronicle*
14 August 1947

'No, no – we want a row over to Paignton, not Palestine'

As already mentioned, tens of thousands of Jewish displaced persons and refugees tried to enter Palestine illegally by boat from Europe. Between August 1946 and May 1948, the British government intercepted more than 50,000 Holocaust survivors seeking to resettle in Palestine.

Frank Hoar 'Acanthus', *News of the World*
31 August 1947

It was becoming clear to the British that little hope existed for a political solution in Palestine. The Arabs were unwilling to accept partition and the creation of a Jewish state. The Palestinian Jews refused to settle for anything less.

Leslie Illingworth, *Daily Mail*
22 September 1947

'And Behold … The Babe Wept'

1111 Marcus Avenue in Lake Success, New York was the temporary location of the United Nations from 1946 to 1951. UNSCOP, the United Nations Special Committee on Palestine, held hearings from September 1947 to decide what course of action to recommend to the UN regarding Palestine.

Victor Weisz 'Vicky', *News Chronicle*
30 September 1947

**'Lay that pistol down, Abie,
Lay that pistol down!
Pistol-packin' Ali,
Lay that pistol down!'**

Australian Minister for External Affairs Dr Herbert Evatt was appointed chairman of another UN committee that was to look directly at the problems facing Palestine. Evatt, despite attempting to appear impartial, strongly favoured partition over UNSCOP's other stated alternative, preferred by the Arab nations, that a single state be formed in the land. Evatt said at the time, 'We really have to choose between recommending a scheme of partition on the one hand and a complete Arabian unitary state on the other; the latter state puts 600,000 Jews at the mercy of the Arabs.' His advocacy saw the partition proposal, with Jerusalem to be administered as an international city, adopted after a vote by his committee. A two-thirds majority of the UN General Assembly, at a meeting chaired by Evatt, then ratified the plan. Callwell Street refers to Arthur Callwell, who was the Australian Minister for Migration.

Ted Schofield, *Sydney Bulletin* (Australia)
8 October 1947

On 11 October 1947, United States Deputy Representative Herschel Johnson convinced the United Nations Assembly to agree to the partition of Palestine: 'If we are to effect through the United Nations a solution to this problem, it cannot be done without the use of the knife.' Fellow American Ben Hecht was the highest-paid screenwriter in Hollywood, but in his spare time he wrote fiery newspaper ads denouncing Britain's Palestine policy.

Leslie Illingworth, *Daily Mail*
13 October 1947

The Promised Land

Hugh Hutton,
Philadelphia Inquirer
(United States)
1 December 1947

Peace Omen

Bruce Russell,
Los Angeles Times
(United States)
2 December 1947

The United Nations General Assembly voted in favour of the partition of Palestine into separate Jewish and Arab states, with Jerusalem as an international city. Voting was thirty-three for and thirteen against, with ten nations, including Britain, abstaining. Iraq, Saudi Arabia, Syria, Pakistan and Yemen all declared they would not feel themselves bound by the decision, and reserved the right to take whatever action they deemed fit.

One Bird's Folly Is Another's Meat

There were fears in Washington that Russia was using the civil war in Palestine as a pretext for sending Soviet troops into Palestine to fill the vacuum after the British left, and thereby establish a strategic hold in the Middle East and threaten the US Arabian oilfields and the Suez Canal. William C. Bullitt, former US ambassador in Moscow, said: 'If we should permit Stalin to control Western Europe, modern Soviet planes, based on the Continent, could establish the first effective blockade of Britain in history.'

Arthur Poinier, *Detroit Free Press* (United States)
2 December 1947

Although the United Nations had assumed responsibility for Palestine, British troops were responsible for peacekeeping. On 1 December, the United Nations had accepted the idea of partitioning Palestine into two zones, one for the Jews (Israel) and the other for the Arabs (Palestine). Resolution 181 of the UN General Assembly supported the proposal. Inevitably, the new Israeli state was immediately criticised by the surrounding Arab nations, who walked out of the UN in protest.

Leslie Illingworth, *Daily Mail*
2 December 1947

British policy in Palestine. Where are we, Ernie?

On 26 September, British Colonial Secretary Arthur Creech Jones had announced the decision to end the Palestine mandate, thereby handing over responsibility to the United Nations. Ernest Bevin reiterated Britain's reluctance to take responsibility for the results of the United Nations General Assembly's decisions. British troops and the British administration, Bevin declared, would in no circumstances be used to enforce such decisions against either Jews or Arabs.

Victor Weisz 'Vicky', *News Chronicle*
2 December 1947

The Shriek of Araby

George White,
Tampa Tribune
(United States)
3 December 1947

Miracle Man

Sam Wells,
Melbourne Herald
(Australia)
4 December 1947

The Arab League had rejected the United Nations decision to partition Palestine, on the basis that in addition to the Arabs forming a two-thirds majority, they owned a majority of the lands. They also indicated an unwillingness to accept any form of territorial division, arguing that it violated the right to national self-determination. They therefore resolved to resist at all costs the creation of separate Jewish and Arab states.

One Against the World

Daniel Fitzpatrick,
St. Louis Post Dispatch
(United States)
4 December 1947

First Crack

After the United Nations had approved the partition of Palestine, the violence between Jews and Arabs escalated. Tensions rose as sporadic outbreaks of rioting by Arabs increased. A consequence of the violence was the decision by the Haganah, the Jewish paramilitary organisation, to use force in order to stop further attacks on Jews. The British began to relax their control over the country as the date for their departure drew near, and the fighting intensified.

George Butterworth, *Daily Dispatch*
4 December 1947

'I See the Old Homestead and Faces I Love'

Despite the implication here that British troops were all but waiting to be evacuated, Britain had warned both Arabs and Jews that its armed forces intended to continue to enforce law and order in Palestine until control of the mandate had come to an end. The Palestine government, Creech Jones said, would 'take the necessary action to prevent a conflict. The Arab leaders have been told this.' The Argyll and Sutherland Highlanders moved into the no man's land between Jewish Tel Aviv and Arab Jaffa, where there had been many clashes. Despite this action by the British, there was fighting between men armed with tommy guns and grenades.

Ian Gall, *News of the World*
7 December 1947

Ernest Bevin informed American Secretary of State George Marshall of the British plans for withdrawal from Palestine and of the difficulties expected if the UN Commission should arrive in Palestine more than two weeks before the British were ready to hand over authority to the Commission. Bevin expressed the hope that the US would not exacerbate the situation by encouraging illegal Jewish immigration to Palestine.

Leslie Illingworth, *Daily Mail*
10 December 1947

Symbol of the Holy Land

According to the cartoonist: 'The struggle for independence continued in the Middle East. The sword of death was the new symbol in Palestine, where Jews fought to reclaim their ancient homeland.'

Ross A. Lewis, *Milwaukee Journal* (United States)
23 December 1947

NEW CHAPTER OF TRIBULATION

On 30 December 1947, in Haifa, members of the Irgun threw two bombs into a group of Arab workers who were queueing in front of a refinery, killing six and injuring forty-two. An incited crowd murdered thirty-nine Jews in a revenge attack, until British soldiers were able to re-establish order.

David Low, *Evening Standard*
2 January 1948

Despite the British and American arms embargo on Palestine, both the Jews and the Arabs sought to bolster their forces by importing arms. In contravention of the embargo, the Jews received arms shipments from Czechoslovakia and the Soviet bloc, consisting of tanks, armoured cars, artillery and aircraft.

Leslie Illingworth, *Daily Mail*
14 January 1948

Sands of the Times

Uncle Sam: 'Guess I've got my own sand and I'm sticking to it.'

Britain refused to join an America-sponsored 'Big Five' Committee to solve the UN dilemma on how it could impose partition of Palestine when Britain surrendered the mandate on 15 May. Arthur Creech Jones, the British Colonial Secretary, said that Britain could not join such a committee and that there could be no hope that she might keep her troops in Palestine any longer than the August deadline already set. He then gave this warning: 'Whatever procedure the United Nations may decide to adopt with a view to assuming responsibility for the Government of Palestine on 15 May, that country is likely to become disorganised, disintegrated and even more violent and disrupted on that date.'

George Middleton, *Birmingham Gazette*
4 March 1948

"FELLOW-TRAVELLERS, HUH?"

The Arab League refused to cooperate in any way with the five-nation United Nations Commission on Partition. Arab armies began to prepare themselves for the use of force against the creation of a Jewish state.

David Low, *Evening Standard*
5 March 1948

'IF YOU KNOW OF A BETTER HUMP ...'

Changing Mounts in Mid-Stream

The United States withdrew its support for the United Nations General Assembly's partition proposals and proposed, instead, a temporary trusteeship regime for Palestine. Russia opposed such a plan. Andrei Gromyko told the Security Council at Lake Success that the proposal for trusteeship would not eliminate the difficulties which had arisen in implementing partition. Gromyko maintained that partition of Palestine into independent Jewish and Arab states was a just solution.

George Middleton, *Birmingham Gazette*
23 March 1948

Trespassers Will Be Murdered

The *Daily Worker* slavishly followed the Soviet Union's line on Palestine, which saw the American proposal of trusteeship as 'a new American plan to complete the sell-out of the Palestinian Jews to the oil interests'. It is interesting to note that the far left have always seen Middle Eastern policy as dictated by oil. In later conflicts the Arab populations were seen by them as pawns in the hands of the oil interests. For the communists of the 1940s, it was the Jews.

Jimmy Friell 'Gabriel', *Daily Worker*
24 March 1948

Dangerous Potion …

The cartoon alludes to the Russian expression 'to stir porridge', meaning 'to stir up trouble'.

Boris Efimov, *Izvestia* (Soviet Union)
25 March 1948

'I don't want her, you can have her, she's too fat for me'

Ernest Bevin stated that whatever now occurred in Palestine, Britain was definitely leaving on 15 May: 'Why should the British Government be blamed? We are blamed when we try to get out. We are blamed for what might happen when we get out. I think the quicker we get out the better. Another situation could and might arise. … We have made up our minds very strongly that we cannot be in the same position as the rest of the members of the United Nations until we are out of Palestine.'

Sidney Moon, *Sunday Dispatch*
28 March 1948

The 'Cat' that Came Back

According to the *Gloucester Journal*: 'The racial struggle, the blood vendetta, the mass murders in Palestine continue unabated. In fact the tempo indeed accelerates and meanwhile the United Nations Organisation continues to debate the position, with nothing tangible done. The United States, faced with the consequences of her own action in withdrawing support for the partition plan, has launched a new plea to the Security Council. She wants a special meeting of the Assembly to call for an immediate truce in Palestine and then to consider the future government of the Holy Land. As was to be expected Russia had said "No" to this and the Assembly is at once torn into two schools diametrically opposed. Meanwhile 15 May draws steadily nearer and the position, once Britain ends her mandate, is fraught with direful possibilities.'

George Middleton, *Birmingham Gazette*
31 March 1948

He Looks to Us – His Only Hope

Most Holocaust survivors felt there was no future for them in Europe. After the Second World War, 250,000 Jewish refugees were stranded in displaced persons camps in Europe. Despite the pressure of world opinion, the British refused to lift the ban on immigration and admit Jews into Palestine. Conditions in the Cyprus detention camps and the sight of Holocaust survivors being held behind barbed wire also stirred widespread criticism of British handling of the problem of Jewish immigration to Palestine.

D. Liebman, *The Jewish Exponent* (United States)
2 April 1948

Warsaw–Palestine: The Battle Continues

Inspired by the resistance shown by the Jews in the Warsaw ghetto, the Jewish army, soon to be known as the IDF (Israel Defence Forces), formed from the merger of the Haganah and some members of the terrorist Irgun and Stern gangs, began the major phase of the battle for Palestine on the eve of the Jewish Feast of Passover. By means of a surprise assault they managed to capture strategic positions in the main seaport of Haifa.

Artist unknown, *Jewish Advocate* (United States)
22 April 1948

This Year –Next Year – Sometime –?

Arthur Creech Jones insisted that Britain was determined to withdraw the last of her forces from Palestine by the beginning of August: 'It has been no easy task in these recent months for our diminishing Forces. Yet in discharge of their duties, in the interest of Arabs and Jews alike, they have been brutally attacked and often savagely murdered. Since the partition resolution was passed 130 British soldiers and police have been killed, more than 300 wounded and most vile atrocities have been committed against them by Jewish terrorists. I utterly deny that the administration has not been impartial. Theirs has been a thankless and most difficult task.'

J.C. Walker, *Western Mail*
24 April 1948

Save The Holy Places

The threat of a Soviet veto to the American proposal for a temporary trusteeship over Palestine instead of partition occurred when Andrei Gromyko accused America of abandoning the agreed partition solution because the US wanted to 'convert Palestine into a military strategic base of the United States'. He went on to say that responsibility for wrecking partition fully rested on the United States, 'which was putting oil and strategic interests before United Nations interests'.

Herbert Block 'Herblock', *Washington Post*
(United States)
27 April 1948

Count Folke Bernadotte was sent by the United Nations Security Council to try to negotiate a settlement between the Arabs and Jews in Palestine. However, his proposals for a sustainable solution to the conflict were rejected outright by both sides. In September, Bernadotte was assassinated in Jerusalem by members of the Lehi Jewish underground gang.

Leslie Illingworth, *Daily Mail*
28 April 1948

'The Wall Fell Down Flat'

The Arab states rejected the plea by the United Nations Truce Committee in Jerusalem to discuss peace in Palestine.

George Butterworth, *Daily Dispatch*
28 April 1948

Real Politiks

Andrei Gromyko, the Soviet representative to the United Nations, declared that the United States had killed partition because it had 'put all its strategic interests before United Nations interests'. Senator Warren Austin called for an immediate truce in Palestine, believing partition would lead to civil war and the likelihood that the Soviets would supply military assistance to Israel.

Jimmy Friell 'Gabriel', *Daily Worker*
28 April 1948

'Wailing Wall'

Arab armies prepared to cross the Palestine border and invade the Holy Land. King Abdullah of Jordan predicted that 'Operation Palestine' would tighten the ring around the Jewish enemy. A message from the Haganah, the Zionist defence force, had noted that Syrian and Lebanese armoured forces had invaded at dawn, and had encircled three Jewish settlements in the Upper Galilee. The Haganah also announced: 'This is the first outright invasion of Palestine by armies of neighbouring Arab States.'

Jacob Burck, *Chicago Sun-Times*
(United States)
2 May 1948

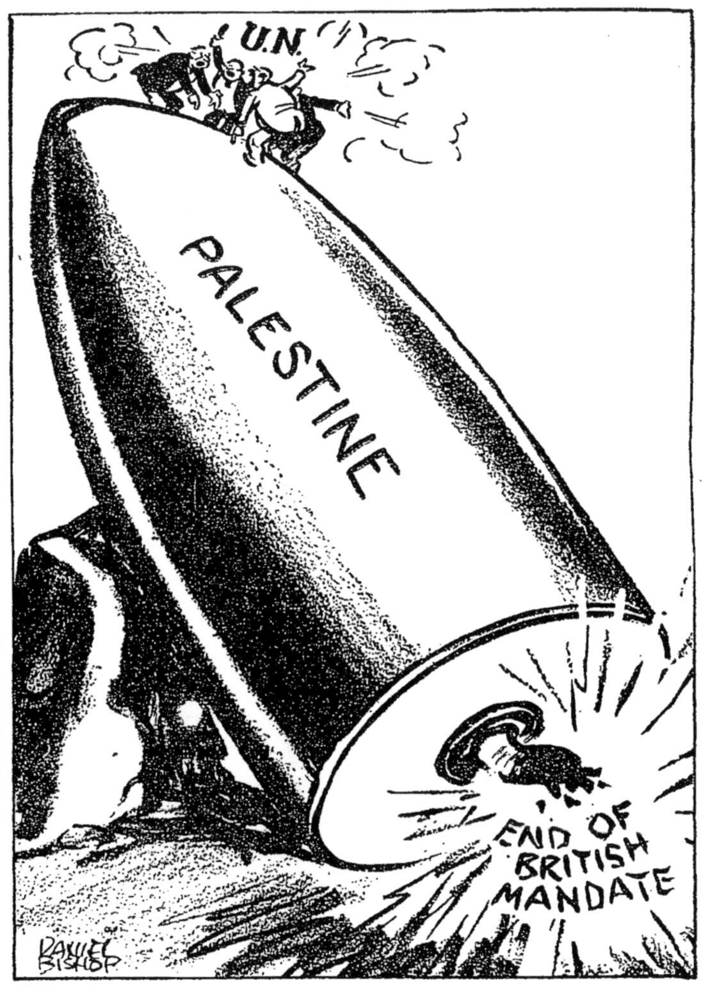

'The Argument's About to End'

According to Reuters, the French newspaper *L'Époque* blamed the United Nations partition scheme for the war in Palestine: 'The desperate efforts at Lake Success to bring about a truce are like those of a person with an umbrella who tries to stop two people fighting with machine guns.' The paper added: 'As for Russia, she is playing the old game of Anglophobia: she attacks the Arab League, but encourages the nationalism of the people who follow it.' The left wing *Franc-Tireur* said: 'It is America and Britain who can do everything, who have all the means to make the medieval petty kings and the Fascists of the Arab League see reason. Are America and Britain going to allow Jewish and Arab blood to continue to flow?'

Daniel Bishop, *St. Louis Star-Times*
(United States)
2 May 1948

Arab from the Tribe of Warmongers

'The so-called Arab Legion, active in Palestine by the order of King Abdullah of Transjordan, is paid by the British.' (From newspaper reports.) King Abdullah of Jordan is seen signing a document entitled: 'Order to the Arab Legion on its combat mission in Palestine'.

On 4 May, King Abdullah, as part of his effort to seize as much of Palestine as possible, sent in the British trained and funded Arab Legion to attack Israeli settlements.

Mark Abramov 'Moa', *Pravda* (Soviet Union)
6 May 1948

With five days until the end of the mandate, the *New York Times* reported that the British government had asked the United Nations Palestine Commission for assurances on the protection of British economic interests in Palestine. This included the oil pipeline from Iraq to Haifa after the British mandate ended.

Leslie Illingworth, *Daily Mail*
10 May 1948

Cop on a Kiddie Car

Jews and Arabs at the UN Assembly at Lake Success reacted to the plan for an interim United Nations authority with certain administrative functions for the whole of Palestine. Having taken responsibility for partition, the United Nations did not have the ability to enforce its outcome or prevent the predicted likelihood of war.

John Collins, *Montreal Gazette* (Canada)
12 May 1948

Two's Company

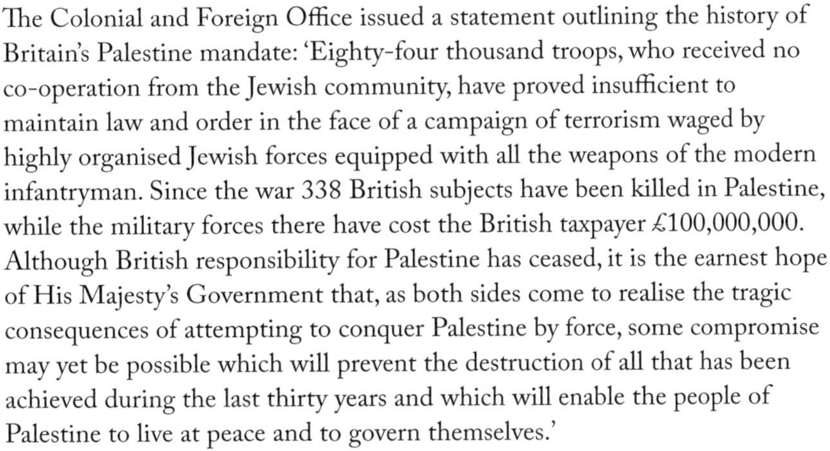

The Colonial and Foreign Office issued a statement outlining the history of Britain's Palestine mandate: 'Eighty-four thousand troops, who received no co-operation from the Jewish community, have proved insufficient to maintain law and order in the face of a campaign of terrorism waged by highly organised Jewish forces equipped with all the weapons of the modern infantryman. Since the war 338 British subjects have been killed in Palestine, while the military forces there have cost the British taxpayer £100,000,000. Although British responsibility for Palestine has ceased, it is the earnest hope of His Majesty's Government that, as both sides come to realise the tragic consequences of attempting to conquer Palestine by force, some compromise may yet be possible which will prevent the destruction of all that has been achieved during the last thirty years and which will enable the people of Palestine to live at peace and to govern themselves.'

J.C. Walker, *Western Mail*
14 May 1948

'Not Like Dachau, Is It, Herr Mufti?'

The Grand Mufti, al-Hajj Amin al-Husseini, who had instigated Arab revolts in Palestine in 1929 and 1936, had fled to Germany in 1941 after being chased out of Iraq. There he was paid to make anti-British radio broadcasts to the Middle East and urge Arabs to attack Allied forces and kill Jews. He met Hitler and tried to persuade him to extend the Nazis' anti-Jewish programme to the Middle East. In 1942, he infamously visited Trebbin concentration camp.

Bernard Seaman, *New York Times* (United States)
14 May 1948

Zero Hour

On the day this cartoon was published, Israel declared its independence. The next day, the British Army departed from Palestine, leaving the Jews and the Arabs to fight it out. The fighting intensified as forces from neighbouring Arab states joined the Palestinian Arabs in attacking territory in the former Palestine mandate. The armies that attacked Israel were those of Syria, Lebanon, Iraq, Saudi Arabia, Egypt and Jordan. For all their numerical superiority, the Arabs were ill-equipped, inexperienced and unprepared.

Sam Wells, *Melbourne Herald* (Australia)
14 May 1948

'There'll be some commotion this side of the ocean, they can't blame us now – BLESS 'EM ALL'

The cartoon's caption is an allusion to a popular Second World War song, 'The Long and the Short and the Tall', and strongly implies that Britain was relieved to be able to wash its hands of Palestine. In the end, British rule and policies had met with the approval of neither the Arabs nor the Jews.

Sidney Moon, *Sunday Dispatch*
16 May 1948

The Only Bloom

The United States was the first country to recognise Israel when President Truman issued a statement of recognition following Israel's proclamation of independence just eleven minutes earlier. Three days later, with Stalin believing that the new Jewish state might be a useful thorn in the side of Britain and the United States, the Soviet Union followed suit.

George White, *Tampa Tribune* (United States)
20 May 1948

'And apart from not telling me, it doesn't look like mine!'

According to the *Daily Worker*: 'The *Manchester Guardian* put the matter bluntly in a leading article entitled "In The Wrong": "In the last few days our relations with the United States have deteriorated shockingly. Britain is held to be playing a dishonest game in Palestine and to be assisting and subsidising the Arabs to defy United Nations policy. This view is held not only in America but all over the continent; for once, anti-Communist and Communist speak alike; Americans and Russians are on the same side."'

Jimmy Friell 'Gabriel', *Daily Worker*
23 May 1948

Behind the Arab Aggression in Palestine: Arabian tricks of Mr Bevin

Boris Efimov, *Izvestia* (Soviet Union)
25 May 1948

Non-Intervention

Jimmy Friell 'Gabriel', *Daily Worker*
25 May 1948

The British government continued to subsidise the Jordanian Army with money, arms and British officers in the face of public opinion both at home and abroad. According to the *Daily Worker*: 'Faced with the fact that the Jewish forces are gaining the upper hand in the military struggle, King Abdullah of Transjordan is sending reinforcements to his Arab Legion already in Palestine … There can be no doubt that this action of Abdullah is equivalent to a British declaration of war on the Jews, for this King is nothing but a British puppet, his forces are led by British officers and he receives for their upkeep a subvention of £2 million a year from the Treasury. We are witnessing in Palestine Mr Bevin's final throw of the dice in order to prevent a peaceful solution of the problem there …'

'Here I Am – You STILL Can't Recognise Me?'

Bevin opposed the creation of a Jewish state in Palestine because he was convinced it would have a damaging effect on Britain's extensive interests in the Middle East. He continued to withhold recognition of Israel until its borders were settled, and refused to support Israel's application for membership of the United Nations.

Victor Weisz 'Vicky', *News Chronicle*
14 July 1948

By August, Israel had defeated all the Arab states that had attacked it. The country had grown well beyond the original partition lines. It had also gained more defensible borders and by destroying Arab villages had further reduced the Palestinian Arab population.

Leslie Illingworth, *Daily Mail*
12 August 1948

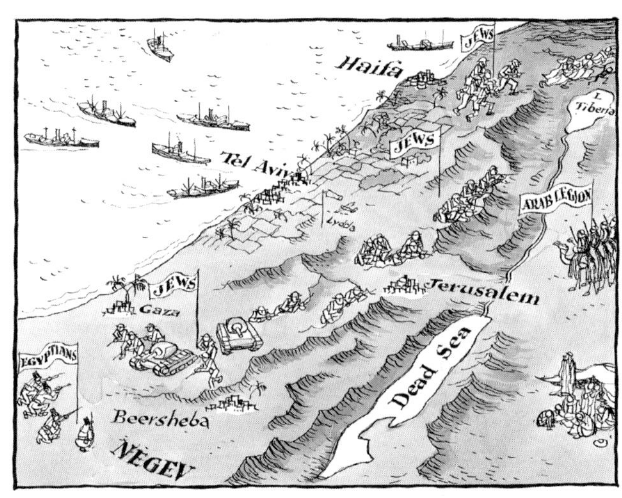

According to the *Scotsman*: 'The Political Committee of the UN General Assembly will not resume its debate on Palestine until after the American Presidential election. Such, apparently, is the course at present preferred by the US delegation, who, after supporting early British wishes to have the Palestine question given precedence over all others, now strongly reinforce the marked reluctance in other quarters to come to grips with Count Bernadotte's proposals for a settlement. From the US standpoint, it would no doubt be desirable to avoid having partisan sentiment running high on the eve of the election.'

Leslie Illingworth, *Daily Mail*
1 November 1948

O Say, Can't You See?

According to the cartoonist: 'A new state was being born in Palestine. A resolution of the General Assembly of the United Nations had recommended in 1947 the partition of Palestine into two independent states – Arab and Jewish – with Jerusalem and the surrounding territory to be internationalised. The Jewish National Council in Palestine, at the termination of the British Mandate, proclaimed on 14 May 1948 the establishment of the new Jewish state to be called Israel. Its admission to United Nations membership was postponed until peace and more definite frontiers had been established.'

Daniel Fitzpatrick, *St. Louis Dispatch*
(United States)
17 November 1948

Recognition

A Possible Scene in the Bulrushes

Although the Attlee government survived a parliamentary vote of confidence on Palestine, 150 Labour MPs joined the opposition or abstained. As a consequence, Bevin became reconciled to the idea of a Jewish state. On 29 January 1949, eight months after the proclamation of the state of Israel, he granted it de facto recognition.

Leslie Illingworth, *Punch*
2 February 1949

According to the cartoonist: 'An armistice in Palestine was negotiated with the help of a United Nations mediator. The ancient dream of a Jewish Home in Palestine had materialised in the State of Israel, achieved, however, not in peace and goodwill as had been hoped, but through a successful campaign of terrorism and assassination followed by war. Friends who had striven in the past for justice to the Jewish people were now uneasily doubtful whether complete justice had been done to the Arabs.'

David Low, *Evening Standard*
4 February 1949

According to the *Yorkshire Evening Post*: 'Ernest Bevin, who in 1945 staked his reputation on finding a solution of the Palestine problem, cut a very poor figure in last night's debate and was justly castigated by Mr Churchill. His failure has indeed been "gross and glaring", and has led to a vast waste of money, repeated loss of British lives and humiliation of every kind.' In the debate Churchill had accused Bevin of 'astoundingly mishandling' the Palestine problem, declaring: 'His Palestine plight is indeed melancholy. No one ever made such sweeping declarations of confidence in himself on this point as Mr Bevin and nobody has been proved by events more continually wrong at every turning point and every moment than he has.'

Jimmy Friell 'Gabriel', *Daily Worker*
17 January 1949

On 7 January 1949, the United Nations announced an Israeli-Egyptian ceasefire in Palestine. The ceasefire was followed by armistice negotiations between the two governments under UN chairmanship. Hard negotiations led to the signing of a truce by both parties by the end of February 1949. As Egypt was the leading Arab nation, it paved the way for later agreements between Israel and Jordan, Lebanon and Syria.

Ross A. Lewis, *Milwaukee Journal* (United States)
26 February 1949

According to the cartoonist: 'Nine hundred thousand Palestinian Arab refugees camped in miserable conditions over the frontier limit of the new State of Israel posed a formidable problem for international relief organisations to cope with. Jews abroad, with memories of the past of their race, thought that Ben Gurion and Moshe Sharett of the Israeli government should take the opportunity to make a gesture of compassionate sympathy. But Israel had little money and was already overcrowded by the tidal wave of new immigrants.'

David Low, *Evening Standard*
23 March 1949